DRIFTWOOD PRESS

EDITORS

CREDITS

Independently published by *Driftwood Press*
in the United States of America.

Fonts: Satellite, Garamond, Cinzel, League Gothic,
& Merriweather.
Cover Image & Content Illustrations: Kelsey M. Evans
Cover Design: Sally Franckowiak
Magazine Design: James McNulty

Published in January 2021
ISSN Print: 2578-7195
ISSN Online: 2331-7132
ISBN-13: 978-1-949065-09-1

Please visit our website at www.driftwoodpress.net
or email us at editor@driftwoodpress.net.

ISSUE 8.1

Table of

Contents

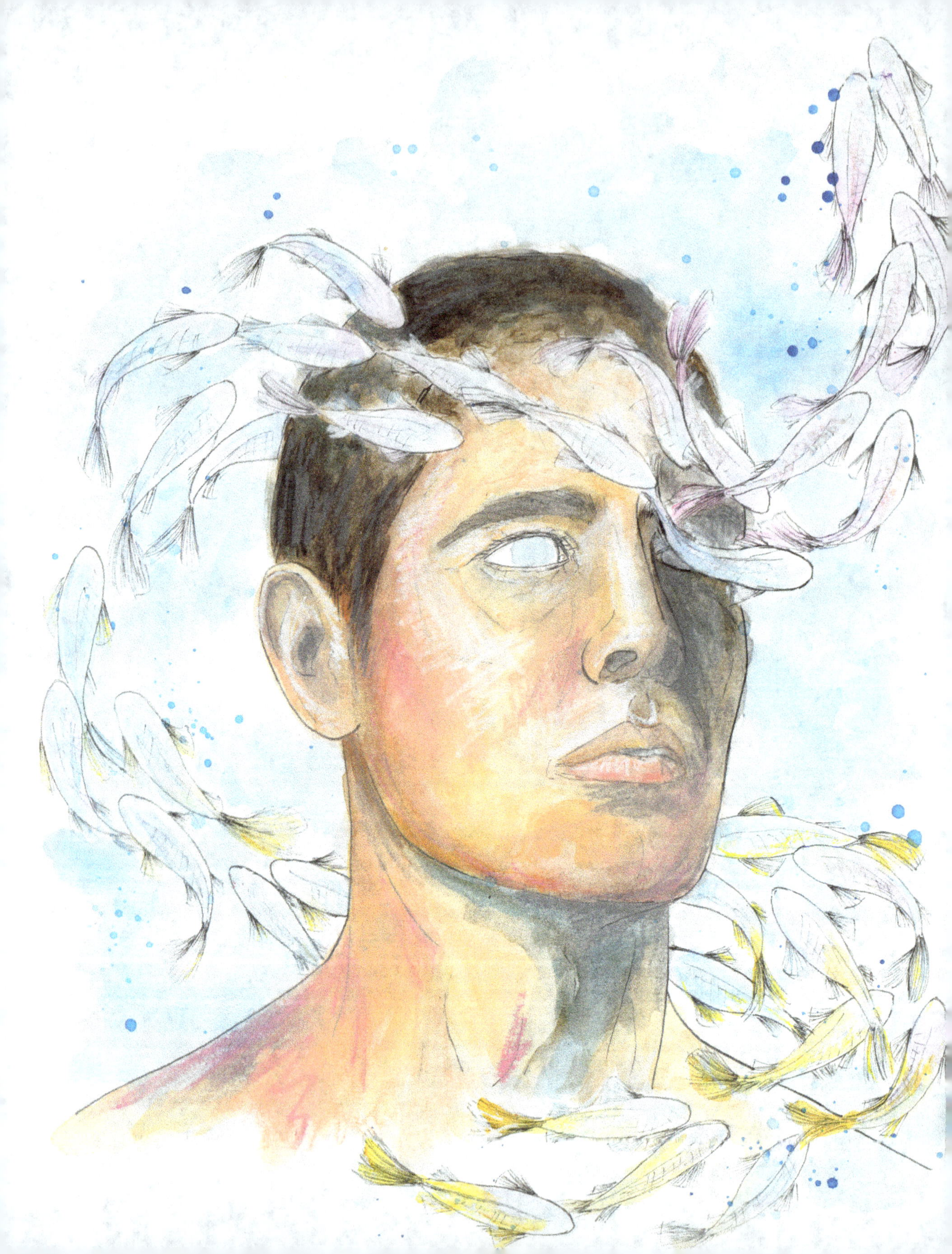

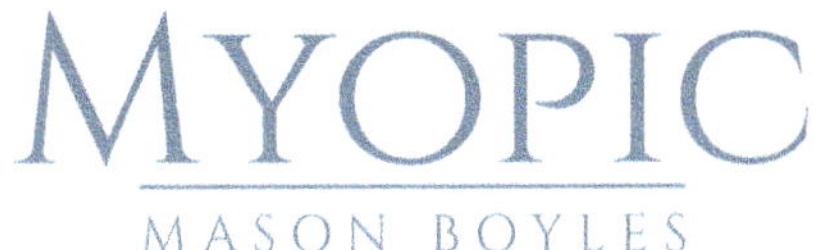

MYOPIC

MASON BOYLES

In Daen Lao's lowest rhizomes even air feels like limestone. The same tectonics inching foothills higher compress emptiness to diamond density; underground—past the bats, and the tombs, and the stalagmites like so many teeth—past the point where absence grows thick, dark becomes wetness, a presence on your skin. A current pulling Gower lower. Closer.

Only once has he stood in it. He'd groped down until slick fish puckered past, mouths suctioning bodies pruned by their home's sparseness, flanks colorless the way moonlight is colorless, as though color was only imposed by his looking. Everything was imposed by Gower's looking, the stream and rock raw in his flashlight as though arranged by its beam.

Later, visiting zoologists would explain: optic atrophy. What began as a dulling had extended to lids that grew shut, nerves that withered until even darkness disappeared. That night in the cave Gower had watched the fish for so long he'd gone senseless himself—no idea which way he'd descended from—and there'd been a strange relief in that moment. A kind of inertia. If Sadie's voice hadn't bounced down to him then, he might've stayed until his own pupils raisined in his skull. He wouldn't have been the first to join those sightless fish.

Twenty years later, Gower still longs for that low. When the world waxes vernal and Tham Lod fumes with the haze of combusted bamboo, he takes out the bowl he keeps under his desk. He puts his face to the glass and watches the cavefish dart and sink. They aren't blind, he's decided. Sight's merely become separate from them, a concept they lack nerves to articulate. Is some yearning preserved in those pinprick bodies? An image scarred codon-deep—light, shade. A loss beyond sensing.

It's the same every spring: Sadie sleepwalks away from him. The lodge crowds with kids on a dozen disparate itineraries—Chang Mai, Burma, the Mekong foothills—faux backpackers, shroomers boasting about ego death. Their stories move through Sadie like a twitch. She starts talking about Full Moon parties in Phuket, hiking south while Aak watches the lodge. Gower sleeps with his arms around her in a Heimlich squeeze, waiting to wake emptyhanded. When he does, he'll take the trail north and find her in the cave.

Her dreams are full-sighted. She told him that once. Though how can she be certain after all these blurred years? Maybe it's her idea of clarity that's fading, her memories narrowing with her vision. He's never asked what she dreams. Does Gower, her life with him, persist when she sleeps? She could be animal, fungal, ancient and wordless, even sedimentary; maybe she's limestone. Once—in dumber years—he'd sat up and followed her. It was a half-mile plunge from the lodge to the cave, a path serrated with roots. She walked barefoot without tripping; feet behind, Gower heard her snoring. He put a hand on her shoulder before she reached the cave. The fallow breath that she drew; how she seemed to spit it back at him. This was the one time she ever spoke Thai to him: mueng, she said, aiming it like accusation. Mueng was what a friend called a friend, or a stranger called a stranger; a word that meant two kinds of you. She aimed it at Gower like an accusation. He gets the feeling she'd slip off from him even if the lodge was empty; that it isn't the kids, or the monsoons, or even the sud-scrub of spring that prompts her sleepwalking. Gower'd like to lose eyes to that. He hasn't tried waking her again. Instead he goes to sleep, wakes to empty, goes to find her spine-stiff a click deep in the cave. She could be a stalagmite, standing that way. A sob still bulges her ribs through her chest when he wakes her. Mueng. She's grieving surfacing, but also—more so—the life that she's surfaced to.

This year it's the Aussie who's stirred her. Phil. He'd coughed down the trail six days back with the wildfire. Been descending Daen Lao, he said. Nearly got caught in the blaze. Gower closed his office door to the rest of the story. He had to narrow the ambience to better interpret Aak, who was explaining how the government sold off destitute land at a hundred baht per acre. Gower's ears were about as waxy as Aak's English. Aak paced in time to his own slanted speech, machete bouncing off the Big Man markings on his legs. Every time he got stuck for words he roosted a hand on the hilt and moved the machete faster, as if the sheathe scraping the markings was flint and wool for his speech. Gower remembered watching those scars cut eighteen years ago—how Aak had seemed to siphon the pain off through his breath, panting it like spent air. Since replacing his father as Tham Lod's Big Man he's led with that same restraint, but the fires were making him manic. This latest was the third burn since June, unheard of for monsoon season. All the flames were concentrated on the fallow slopes southwest of the village. Aak claimed someone was burning down the price on those fields.

"For what?" Gower asked. That land was all rock and root.

Aak slapped his machete off his thigh for a few seconds before drawing it. He laid the blade across the map tacked to the wall, tracing the line between Myanmar and Thailand. He tapped the blade there a second before surrendering English. "Chaydaen," he said. Border.

There was a time when this lodge was more smugglers than backpackers. Traffickers sieved through the cogon like smoke, wafting over the Burma border. But the Shan move all product themselves now; under gunpoint, the province has settled. It's been eighteen years since the village road was last gilled by the Shan's Jeeps—long enough for smugglers to fool themselves brave. Say someone wanted a funnel between Chiang Rai and the refineries. Say they were burning themselves a corridor to buy, cheap, and sneak past the Shan.

It was after midnight when Gower and Aak stepped outside. Phil stood slouched by the trailhead, staring down the slope to the cave.

"It's closed," Gower called. "Tours only."

Phil smoked over their way. His arms were still sooty—or tattoos, those were tattoos. He pointed his cigarette back toward the cave. Dark sealed the jungle, shade clogging the trail between chambers of trees. "Looks open to me."

He's been anchored at the bar ever since. No hiking. No tours. Just smoking, speaking an insistent Strine. Gower still has half a feeling the guy's mocking his own accent; refusing to be baited off the barstool with pho, Phil's sworn he's been chockers since arvo, dinkum. No one speaks like this, not even in Dandenong. He clears the lounge with his long talk and nicotine. It's as if his own insides have combusted. As if, sitting hollow on that stool, he's waiting to be filled with something.

When Gower slogs back from Monday's evening tour and finds Sadie swap-side of the bar, beside Phil, he actually laughs. The guy's backwoods Abercrombie: the Zenzy dreads, the self-shaming references to the real estate firm he's bugged out from—all concentrated character. In two weeks he'll be shaved and suited, back to closings in some Melbourne skyscraper. If he doesn't waft off, that is; he's all string and tendon. As he stoops to his backpack for another box of Krong Thip, his tank top sags low enough to expose a chest stippled with circular burns. Gower's seen those same marks on junkies. They used to nod off in this lounge with smokes lit, drooped cigarettes searing them. The dope necklace—one more thing Sadie can't see. She's rulered on the stool to Phil's right, chewing the cap of her Singha. Gower serves himself and hunkers on

Phil's far side.

"We were talking optics," Phil says. "Font-du-Gaume. You familiar?"

Gower takes that as rhetorical. He's checking out Phil's tattoos—greyscale spirals, curls smoky and painstaking. The ink obscures any track marks, but Phil can't hide his droop. He moves like a falling thing, in muscleless motions.

"There's this cave painting in Indonesia," he's saying. "One way it's a mammoth, but if you squint it turns into a buffalo. World's oldest optical illusion." He tears the front off the Krong Thip carton, the cardstock scarred with a tracheotomy closeup. Since the king made these gruesome warnings mandatory, sales have slowed in the villages but tripled in all the tourist traps—the farangs all get off on death rendered quaintly. The cigarettes crowd the torn carton like that photo's cross-section, the stopped muscles of a neck and throat skinned.

Phil gropes over the far side of the counter for a pen. He smooths the cardstock and sketches a picture inside. Gower watches the lines. A mammoth. A mammoth. Then the image shuffles as he stares. The ears become shoulder blades. Haunches, nostrils. The buffalo appears.

"See?" Phil says. "The drawing's static. It's your brain that changes."

Sadie moves her face close to the picture. Her vision's been worse lately, down to the inches in front of her. Can she see?

"There's a lag between your eyes and your thoughts," Phil explains. "It takes your mind a second to decide what you're seeing. The transformation of translation." He smirks at Gower around his cigarette. "Like a cave."

"How'd you figure?"

"My cousin works rescue for Queensland Petroleum. They had a shaft collapse, then an earthquake. Took three days to dig down to the team. This one bloke was just laying on his ass. They told him to get up and he swore he was already standing. I guess if you go deep enough you lose track of space." Phil's lips crack as he grins. "Ever trip down there?"

"We use headlamps."

"I mean acid. Shrooms."

"You have some?" Sadie asks.

"Thúk yàang. I have everything."

Gower cuts eyes to Sadie, who has a grudge against such flaunts from farang. She ignores anything Gower says in Thai to her. He's fluent, except in his tongue. It always slips the tone between syllables; suAY becomes SUay, so that instead of beautiful he's calling her cursed. But Sadie sits flinchless, as stiffly as if she's just snored through the mouth of that cave.

"We'd get ripper visuals," Phil says, extracting his cigarette as if to swill the smoke in a diagram. "That room with the coal?"

Gower topples his stool when he stands.

Phil puts the cigarette back in his mouth before lifting his hands. "The bird told me."

The last hoon who called Sadie that found a tarantula in his boot. This one gets her reinforcements. "He was asking about fumes on the tours," she says.

Gower rights the stool, but doesn't sit.

"Khian suea hai wua klua." The Thai moves lathered through Phil's lips. Draw the tiger to cattle. A Karen idiom.

As the words grate into place in Gower's head, so does the man; maybe it's the white-collar part of him that's the fiction. Mammoth/buffalo. Gower's been looking, but now he sees.

Phil palm-shaves the frost off the sides of his glass. "How about we shimmy down there and get pissed?"

"Off of what?" Sadie asks.

"Anything. Everything."

Sadie looks to Gower, who looks to Phil, who's clenching the drink to still his hands; the cigarette still trembles in his lips. He's jonesing.

"Sober tours only."

Sadie pushes her stool back. "Gow never learned to dance."

Of course Phil's intrigued her. She's never been able to stand things she hasn't seen for herself. Her Beyondness, Gower calls it. It's the same angst that sends her sleepwalking. She aches up and starts swabbing the bar with a dishrag. She swirls it like a windup—a promise of motion—and Gower knows that tonight he'll wake with empty arms. Maybe this is what sends him to his office for the fishbowl. "Show you something."

Gower sets it on the bar and the creatures wobble up from the bottom, their movement a kind of congealing.

"Strewth," Phil says. "Keep their eggs out me chest."

"What?"

"Alien."

Gower shakes his head.

Sadie speaks over her shoulder. "The movie."

The world these travelers drag their talk from hardly seems real to Gower. He's severed from it, from his folks back in Tas. The nearest phone's an hour east in Chiang Rai, and Gower's stopped making the trip. What if something happens? his Mum'd asked the last time they spoke. Like what? Gower said, knowing she wouldn't word it; still, her question swung back like the Newton's Cradle on her desk at the bodyshop, knocking its own answer back at him. Gower could evaporate in the cogon and she'd keep worrying quotes for insurers. At a distance of half a hemisphere, death and missed calls can't be distinguished.

Phil presses his face to the fishbowl. The creatures blot through the water, gills shuffling, skin strangely plastic. "I'm trying to picture that. Not even knowing what light is."

"Like God," Sadie says.

They both blink at her.

"God's all the things we can't know." She laughs. "I saw that once. A tattoo."

They watch the fish slugging. Gower's thinking of the solid kind of dark, that place where all senses homogenize. He's thinking this doesn't happen in one generation.

Gower first limped into Tham Lod twenty years ago, bleeding and fevered. The heel he'd slashed open on a stray rock in Phayao had festered on his climb through the foothills. He spent six days flat-backed in a phook hut, tended by blonde hallucinations. When his fever broke the visions remained. They were Oli and Rach Maynard, owners of the cave lodge, parents to Sadie. That first conscious night Gower'd writhed awake to find the girl inches from his face.

"Don't move," she said. "I'm almost seeing you."

Her world became watercolor beyond arm's length. Myopia was the proper term, as though it was more a matter of caring than seeing. Some latent gene had been tripped by chronic darkness—her eyes' decline amplified by too much time in the cave. She'd spent her whole life plunging through it. When Gower's heel mended, she pulled him in with her.

That first trip underground was like breathing. In the dark he sensed space in the sudden way one detects their own constant anatomy, the panting and percolating and lactic warble through veins. Movement was different here. Distance a thing you could touch. Following Sadie through the passages Gower felt as though he were slogging through the weight of an extra dimension—the shadows themselves, maybe, crystalizing around them. She explained how the locals had been entering these tunnels for thousands of years. But her parents had flashlights, ropes. They'd gone deeper. Sadie herself had traveled farthest of all, sneaking out of the lodge to repel down until the black seeped into her eyelids.

If there was a door, Oli liked to say, Sadie had to open it; Beyondness had tugged at her, even then. She'd spent her whole life in Tham Lod. As her own vision narrowed she began craving expansion. Gower had empathized. He'd spent a decade painting over dents at his mum's shop in Sorell to save up for a plane ticket. Thailand was the first leg of a galactic walkabout—that's what he'd intended. Then Sadie showed him the throne room.

They had to pinch through a fissure to get there. The fit was so tight it kept Gower from inhaling. He squirmed for ten breathless seconds before the rock stretched its reach. It opened to a cathedral of a cavern. The chamber glinted in their headlamps, the walls argent with strands of anthracite. The roof baroque, all stalactites and limestone buttresses and bats—thousands of bats, squealing frescoes above them. Sadie'd cut her headlamp and raised one hand in front of his. Gower's world honed down to her knuckles, the circled of the beam.

"Now it's equal," she'd said. "You see like I see."

He couldn't help kissing her.

For a moment their mutual future protracted before him: Europe, the Americas, the two of them playing vagabonds. Then he looked up at the shadows clotting, the roof of the cave throbbing with batwings, and the idea inverted. He knew then that Sadie was going to keep him here.

When the Singha is finished they step outside, the three of them, and wade through a night thick as cardboard.

Phil covers his eyes. "I'm bat-like, let me echolocate."

"You feel the soundwaves," Sadie says. "They fly past and it's like a magnet on your skin."

The two of them walk in-step behind Gower. Sadie's head is aimed at Gower's heels, how they used to hike—her navigating by the backs of his boots. Gower turns back to Phil. "How long's the holiday?"

"Holiday?"

"Vision quest. Business trip."

Phil palms Gower's shoulder. He's got big, Swiss Army fingers—the nails jagged, useful for anything. "Reconnoitering." He swivels. "Shit. My backpack."

He jogs back for the lounge, and Gower stomps into a sprint. He hips through the door ahead of Phil and grabs the pack out from under the barstool. It's half-open. A thermos hits the floor rolling when he inverts it. Gower punches the bottom, feeling for hidden pockets. Phil stands silent in the doorway, just watching.

Sadie shoves past him. "Gow! What the hell?"

Gower scoops up the thermos and sniffs. Even sealed, the alcohol stabs his nostrils. He drops it back in the pack and feels it slick on his fingers.

"Ripper," Phil says. "You've seen mine, show me yours. How about that cave tour?"

"Shoot up first." Gower swears he hears Sadie's eyes closing. He snatches at the back of her shirt as she stilts toward the door. "Just don't wake me up when he pulls you out there."

Sadie turns around. "Pull?" she says. Here, a knife-nick of a smile. "Oh, mueng, no one pulls me."

This, what he's feared: that it's not the backpackers, or the monsoons, or even the anthracite that sends her to that cave. The lodge could be empty and she'd still slip away from him. Now it's Gower's eyes closing.

Her kiss hits his cheek like a slap.

He doesn't look till the door slams. Just him and the Aussie now, standing stupidly. Phil sticks his hand out. Gower passes the pack.

The guy's face is laminating, slicking over with sweat. "Nice night for a stroll."

Gower nods. There are leopards in the jungle, and worse things—armed ones. Phil must know this. "Where to?"

Phil's laugh smells like ashes. "Under."

Fine. Let the hoon trip himself. Phil smacks out the door in his thongs.

Gower stands there a long time just to breathe. Rubbing the raw from his lips, he sniffs sweetness. He cups his palm to his face and inhales—it's not alcohol. There's a benzene tinge to the stuff from Phill's thermos, a scent Gower hasn't breathed since the bodyshop. Gasoline.

For two years Gower gave tours. Travelers were always hiking in for the cave. They were coming with heavy backpacks, with sallow eyes and long sleeves and the slow, underwater movements he came to recognize as opiated. Mostly he guided the researchers. Sponging up findings of botanists and geologists, he began to perceive things he'd walked blindly past a hundred times before. There were snails smaller than the space between nailbed and cuticle. Alloy deposits in karsts' crooks, bunched and brindled. A whole world of names: debitage, midden, zospeum tholussum.

The landscape elaborated; so did the Maynards. As Gower and Sadie grew to kudzu-like codependence, she told him what else the cave lodged. There were stashes, she said. Caverns where kilos of dope slicked the floor just like guano. Her parents' role was a blind eye. They'd wanted their hands clean for years, but there was pressure from the refineries. Smugglers needed a safe house between Chiang Rai and the border. The most Oli and Rach had been guilty of was indiscriminate hospitality. The dope market was puckering anyway, the trending substance in the hostels Ya ba. One more summer, Sadie swore. Things would settle, then she and Gower would pack up for Europe. They married agnostically, proximally, their wrists bound with Pook Mue in the Buddhist tradition, and hiked Daen Lao for their honeymoon.

Gower still dreams his way back to the day they returned. He slips through sleep into air like a sigh, the jungle charged with the follow-through of the passing monsoon. The cogon was cold and clingy with rain. They'd spotted Jeep tracks rutting the path to the lodge, dumped their packs and sprinted.

The Shan were all sinew. They paced loose-boned through the courtyard, struggling rifles over their shoulders. Gower pulled Sadie toward the tree line too late; they were spotted, prodded to their knees with the guests and the villagers while soldiers gutted the lodge.

Room by room the place emptied. Oli and Rach never emerged. The sergeant came out of a room with a backpack. He knifed the bottom and the powder spilled free, tea-tinted, falling slow as though stuck to the air's humid molecules. The two travelers dragged to their feet seemed too thin to stand. They wobbled in the soldiers' grips, stares ceramic. How much smack had they swallowed while the Jeeps' engines swelled nearer?

It was strange how Gower hadn't been thinking of Sadie, then; hadn't been thinking at all. How, when the shots bruised through the jungle, the sound reached him as though from above—muffled by distance, dripping shadow. His mind was in the limestone. When he surfaced, the smugglers were still standing. It was Phao, Tham Lod's Big Man, who laid facedown in the mud. The Shan crowded into their Jeeps and drove off and the sky went purple with twilight before anyone moved. The powder had settled on the mud in brown clusters, a million faltered offerings.

From Aak, they gleaned the gist of it: the smugglers had been paying off Oli, who'd been paying off Phao, who'd been paying off the Shan. But the Shan got greedy. They wanted their own hands in the product, so they'd severed the supply chain. Tham Lod had just been cauterized. The Maynards were gone—disappeared. Aak had come up to the lodge that morning to find their room empty.

"They fled," Sadie insisted.

That night was the first time Gower woke to an empty bed. He followed her footsteps to the cave. When he shook her from sleep and she said it again. Fled. Invoking it.

And she kept it up, repeating that claim as the lodge's junkies were replaced with sober backpackers, photographers, film crews from Nature and National Geographic. For all her wanderlust, Sadie couldn't leave Tham Lod while she thought her parents might emerge from the jungle. That thought became habit, a weaker kind of belief. Not that Gower minded. His own imagination had sunken. The one vector he craved was the cave.

He went down and down. He hoarded rope and stripped batteries to silence monoxide monitors. He was chasing that womby warmth where his nerves lost track of his body, where skin and shadow homogenized. There was a shaft in the floor of the throne room that drained to a stream. The fish were from that place. The taxonomists had consulted him for their naming.

Spelaichthys agnōstos. The unknowable.

Gower follows Phil into the courtyard the way fire moves, feeling like a spark chasing after that whiff of gasoline—his pursuit that desperate, that inevitably consuming. The sky seems doused in benzene. Shade seeps into the cloths of Yang Na leaves. He's thinking of Aak slapping his machete to the map, telling him chaydaen; of Sadie in the cave, waiting for Phil to bring her something that'll get them both pissed. Off of what, she'd asked—blind to his track marks. Her Beyondness tugging her again.

Gower stops. He has to let her come back. Needs to know she still wants to. He watches the Aussie darken off through the cogon, then shoves into his room.

The air's weft with her internal, synthetic scent, like semen laced with nicotine. He creaks down on their bed and takes a lung-bulging breath of her and holds it. He wants to be the cavern she crawls into. He traps air until mammoths bend into buffalo behind his eyelids. The buffalo shift again. He gasps standing, picturing her brailling Phil's track marks with her fingers—fixing on it to ward off even darker images.

He runs up the cave trail straining to smell her. The pooled dark of the Daen Lao's entrance. In Mapha dialects the word for shadow is compound, daam-na: 'dark-water.' The blackness of the passage is a kind of wet, Gower thinks. It seems night itself is leaking from the rock. He takes one last breath of clean air and wades in.

A click deep he reaches a molar ledge. They take tours left here, but Gower goes right instead. The rock's fixed with bolt anchors, threaded with a kernmantle to grip. It's a ten-foot tiptoe to the passage Sadie showed him, where he has to go sidewise like a crab. A long pinch through that slit spits him in the throne room.

They used to bring sleeping bags. They'd squeeze through the entrance and spend the night panting into each other, bodies waxing in the anthracite's moony glow. Now Sadie stays clear of the cavern. She claims her vision has worsened, though vision has nothing to do with it; she sleepwalks here, after all. Gower's begun to suspect that he's keeping her out. Something had shifted when he found those fish—he'd penetrated a place she'd never reached. A blindspot.

His presence has tainted a world that was once wholly hers.

Gower spins, watching the coal striate in front of his headlamp. Each deposit glints like a promise; anthracite's highly flammable, another reason they steer tours away—and keep the drugs matchless, like Phil's acid and shrooms. In the near corner of the cavern his light lands on dun. Chimney-stacked packages. He lifts one. The plastic's taut with cavity-colored powder—an airtight brick of dope.

The smack isn't Shan; the hue's not dark enough, it's too pure. Whoever stashed this must've passed the lodge on the way to the cave, and this is the thought that throbs him—they'd been right here, and he'd been oblivious. His chest strains the rock on the squeeze back through the passage. He scrapes along the ledge. He's climbing and panting and thinking of Sadie sleepwalking into crosshairs and something warm smacks his head. A bat returned early from feeding. More beat by, a horde, dragging hot air in their lee. Dropped guano grains his headlamp beam. As the shaft levels, the shade stiffens to smoke. He steps out and sees it like stars on the skyline: the jungle west of Tham Lod detonated in flame.

He trips back up the path, stubbing toes. The wind slaps him with smoke, but also the sound of it: the jungle burns with a ramping hum, like the smoke-strands are pistons. It's swelling this way.

The courtyard's crowded by the time he gasps into it. A dozen backpackers aim cameras downslope, lenses chomping the blaze. Every asshole with a Nikon's now ANN paparazzi. Gower wheezes to his room and finds it, of course, empty.

How'd he miss her? She should've sleepwalked right into him. He'd have caught her on the path. Passed her in the cave. He runs back out, grabs a girl with an SLR by the strap of it. "Seen Sadie?"

Her lips make a question-shape, another hum dubbing them. Engines.

Two Jeeps fishtail into the courtyard, high beams scything. Before a single order's shouted everyone's on their knees.

The Shan climb out shaking. They drop off the Jeeps' grabs handles and step bars, in five shades of camo; some wear printed cargo shorts, t-shirts for fatigues. Their shoulders droop with the weight of their rifle straps. The crooks of their elbows are snakebitten with bruise. Soldiers will march for money. They'll shoot for ideals. But for dope—if they've tasted it—they'll impale themselves. They'll starve clicks through the jungle to fire on their own families. Gower raises his arms in time with their rifles, swearing himself in a dream.

The sergeant is least-dressed, last to exit. He has to jump down from the driver's side. He lands barefoot, flak vest sliding low on his coat hanger clavicles, and the Shan slap their brows in salute. On his neck—pointing up—is his ranking, three chevrons nooked and stacked in tattoos. They stretch gill-like when he speaks. "We intend no hurt further," he says, and each word is pruned perfect, practiced over—the chalkboard English of boarding schools. "We must say with the proprietor. Speak."

Gower stays kneeling, says nothing. The girl with the SLR points to him. "There!"

The Shan's hands are like children's. They grip Gower as if for support.

"We say in private," the sergeant tells him. He's teenaged, tops, shrunken with smack.

The soldiers go to tiptoes to keep their hands on Gower's shoulders when he stands. He looks down at their lice-pale cowlicks. Shouldn't you be at school? He's inches from asking that.

"We intend no hurt further," the sergeant repeats.

They walk him into the lounge. The soldiers point Gower to a stool. Sitting down, he's still taller. A rifle chills his temple. He sags until the Shan's heads are higher, propping his elbows on his knees, his chin in his hands.

The sergeant spits in his palm at the doorway. He stands on one foot, then the other, slicking mud off his soles. "You must be checking boots, is one thing. You find snakes in. Tarantulas." There's a sealed aspect to his syntax, as if each phrase has been learned as a unit, intact. "You own?"

"Yes."

"Also is there woman?"

Through the window Gower sees the lodge scoured. Doors stripped from hinges, guests crowded in the courtyard, the sky rubberized with smoke. What he hopes—what he pleads—is that Phil left with Sadie. He wants them hitching to Phuket for the Full Moon.

"Fled," Gower says.

Phil's torn carton of Kong Thip is still coastered on the counter. The sergeant bites one by the gilt filter. "The farang thief is present. He wears tattoos."

Gower's looking at the sketch on the cardstock. Mammoth. Buffalo. He looks and he looks, until looking becomes seeing. Of course it's Phil's dope, Phil's the one who planted it. Phil who set the same blaze he stumbled out of, and this one. Destitute land; reconnoitering. Real estate.

"We intend no hurt further," the sergeant says.

Gower points to the trailhead. "I'll show you."

The Shan hate the dark. Gower hears their breaths stiffen as they enter the cave. Their flashlight beams tremble, rifles dropped slack on their straps. He inhales through his nose; below burnsmoke, a menthol's faint scraping. The sergeant's smoking. He's lit a Krong Thip. Gower's throwing his mind south of them. Three clicks past Tham Lod the trail paves, grafting to the one highway in the district. Buy Sadie time, he's thinking. He's thinking she's run for highway; he has to.

Ten minutes. A click. Gower stops sharp at the ledge. The Shan curse softly.

"Through here." He points to the fissure where the kernmantle sprouts like a fuse.

The sergeant lifts his rifle, and for an instant Gower thinks this is it—they'll shoot him, shoot up, no hurt further—but he's gesturing for a soldier to follow. One boy quivers forward. His grip shakes the kernmantle. They slide along the wall scudding pebbles into silt-dark, gripping the ledge with toes flexed through their boots. The soldier's panting against the pinching space. Gower feels like the boy's breath: he funnels into the throne room as dark air, expanding, a presence that shades and penetrates. The soldier follows, spearing his flashlight into the bricks. He calls through the fissure. "Thî nî!"

The Shan squirm and pain into the throne room. As they press toward the stash it occurs to Gower that their shaking isn't fear—it's the smack, tugging at them like gravity. They're pulling out their own shoelaces to tie off with. They're elbow-deep in baggy coat pockets, excavating syringes, spoons. They wrap tarred clots of dope into foil, blind to him. Gower's stretching for the far side of the chamber when the sergeant comes into the room, Krong Thip tucked behind his ear. Its lit tip is still smoking. The walls pulse with a firefly flicker, blued from the cigarette's lifted fumes. Gower slides past him, bending away from his flashlight beam.

It takes no light to find the shaft. Gower steps out of his boots and pees on his bare feet. All water drains downward. He traces his urine where it trickles, like a tightrope—like the ledge—groping that warmth with his toes. They stub on something. He sprawls and strikes softness. Instead of limestone, a lap. Gower pushes up to his elbows. He squints, his rods draining dark like a sieve.

Sadie. She's propped at the mouth of the shaft. Her head lolls with the rock's curve like she's sleeping, only her arm's belted. Gower sneezes brown powder. A brick of heroin is torn open at her feet, the split wrapping as chapped as Phil's sunburnt lips sneering up at him.

Phil'd stashed the smack here. He'd brought it. But it's Gower who's kept her in Tham Lod, bringing her to use it. His need to stay low and close; her waiting for Oli and Rach. Or maybe Sadie was honoring a lower impulse: say she'd been dreaming of dope on all those sleepwalks to this cave. Another part of her Gower's been blind to. Her dope-slowed pulse chars her forearm, browning up her vein like a burnt fuse.

"Phohng khaao!" someone shouts—smack. The cry multiplies behind him like a prayer raised to a chant.

The Shan fumble into the passage. Their flashlights slash as they grope for spoons. The anthracite sprouts vines of light under the angling beams. Gower's voice simmers in his throat. He tries to stand—lunge—but too many of them, they're all pulling out matches. The gagged scrape of one struck; the coal strobes.

It's slow the way falling is slow, the combustion protracted. Gower sprawls onto Sadie even as the flames bloom. Heat overgrows him like kudzu. A pain so high it shifts senses; meat smell, white blindness, river-din.

He stirs beyond his body. His senses gather to him like dew, clinging to his shape without entering his skin. And he cannot see, cannot feel, cannot stand Sadie under him. She's as closed to him as dark and rock, his shielding of her that as futile. The Shan cracked, stalagmitic, moaning. Gower follows the water, the line of that stream. He crawls down the shaft. Slithers. Sightless. Sadie. He'll always be meung to her.

Their first night in the throne room they'd sexed themselves to sleep. Sweating, clutching—that time she'd been the one who woke empty-armed. Gower had dreamed down this shaft and woken somewhere deeper, no idea how he'd come. A parched dark. A stream. He'd cupped up a handful of water and there it was: the face without eyes, the fish's gills flexing. Something else past his headlamp beam. Bone. Two skeletons parted the stream.

Sadie's voice had rattled down to him and he'd climbed back up, he'd shown her the fish trapped in his thermos. Eighteen years she'd been waiting for her parents, Gower never telling her that he'd found them.

Now he swims for deeper dampness. Sleek bodies begin passing him, pinching his legs. Toothless mouths chewing. Gower isn't thinking of Phil. He's not thinking of Oli or Rach, or his own mother, or even Sadie. As he trickles through the stream—dissolves in it—he's thinking of that bowl under his desk, the fish lazing there: mouths groping, searching, starving, going still. Senseless. Undetected.

Free.

BLINDSPOTS

A CONVERSATION WITH MASON BOYLES

The following conversation was conducted by managing fiction editor James McNulty.

James McNulty: Hey, Mason! Congrats on winning our annual Adrift Short Story Contest! Geronimo Johnson picked your story from a handful of finalists. What did he have to say about "Myopic" when he called you?

Mason Boyles: Thanks, James! I was delighted to get the call from Geronimo, and grateful for the generous time he took speaking with me. We talked about the importance of voice as a point of entry in short fiction; a writer creates a world for the reader out of language, and the more distinct and consistent that language feels, the more coherent that world becomes, bringing us closer to the narrator or the consciousness of the POV character.

JM: Great way to jump into it—I'm not surprised that Geronimo spoke on this. I think the most striking element of this story is its extreme—almost alienating—specificity, or, as you say, "the distinct and consistent language" that makes the world "coherent" and brings us closer to an accurate, realized consciousness of a character. We can tackle this huge discussion from a number of ways, but let's start with the logistics: the research. Could you talk a little about the amount of research that went into this story? How'd you nail down Thai vernacular, politics, and culture?

MB: The impetus for this story came from a conversation with an Aussie ex-pat who runs a 'cave lodge' in northern Thailand. He spoke frankly about the heroin trafficking in the area and the local tensions with Thai authorities and the Shan Army. That gave me my setting and context. I always try to follow character rather than research into a story, so I began with Gower and Sadie and sought out the geology, zoology, politics, and linguistics as needed.

The setting, the cave lodge, and the heroin stash were all inspired by the ex-pat. I spent a lot of time watching travel videos to get a visual sense of Northen Thailand, then dove into some heavier geological and botanical reading to familiarize myself with the taxonomies through which Gower would see it. It was important to me that my research was always in service of occupying his character more closely. Gary Snyder writes about the intimacy we gain with nature when we name it, and part of Gower's fascination with Daen Lao seemed to derive from his 'late acquisition' of its particular terminology. He had to work to achieve fluency in a landscape that the locals know intuitively, and I think that he sees this divide as something that's keeping him from Sadie. It took me a good bit of historical reading to understand the political context surrounding the northern border disputes, child soldiers, and the Shan Army. I've never written a story that required so much preliminary research. I rarely write so far from my own experience, but that ex-pat's story stuck in my mind, so it became necessary to take the time. I wrote the first scene of this story in May of 2017, and the story went through a number of drawer-ings, stallings, and drafts before I felt confident enough with the characters and material to land on the ending.

JM: May 2017—sounds about right. The clear effort in this story—on both the sentence level and the research—is clear to see. I'm not surprised it took you so long; the effort was clearly worth it—the result stuns. Do you think this amount of research will be the new norm? Or, if not, how has writing this story changed future drafting for you?

MB: I sure hope this kind of research won't become the norm, but it's proving to be. Right now I'm revising a novel that brushes up against the development of the North Carolina highway systems, a fictionalized, southernized version of the Pennsylvania-Dutch practice of Braucha, and the Appalachian coal mining industry—none of which I was familiar with when I wrote the first scene. I've done a lot of technical reading about strip mining methods and machinery for just a few peripheral passages, but that research was necessary to fully occupy the world of the story. Even details that don't appear on the page put me closer to the turf that my characters are moving through, which is critical for me to write forward confidently.

JM: Makes sense to me; the best way to understand a person is to put yourself in their shoes, as the saying goes. Researching the character's day-to-day inevitably results in more confident prose and a more realized character. Could you share a little bit about the drafting process? Did you work to outline this story and research it simultaneously, or did you research as you wrote?

MB: I researched as I wrote, only turning to the books when something was going to show up in a scene. I always separate research from writing time (I keep dedicated writing hours in the morning and save the background reading for later in the day). When something I hadn't anticipated made its way into in my first draft of "Myopic," like the anthracite in the throne room, I 'wrote around' that scene and moved on, then came back and wrote in the coal seams later.

JM: The fact that you have time set aside for "background reading" says quite a bit; I wish more writers and submitters took this approach and properly acknowledged the amount of research necessary to steep your world in specificity. For readers who aren't familiar with the Shan and Thailand politics, could you give us a little primer?

MB: I only schedule research time because I have to! If I didn't, I wouldn't ever get to it (another reason this story took so long to complete). It's more painstaking and less rewarding than writing, but as you say: necessary. The Shan State Army originated as an insurgent group in 1960s Myanmar, originally recruiting and training locals to combat government forces. They wound up opposing CIA-sponsored soldiers, the Burmese Communist Party, and opium smugglers, and the organization was disbanded in the late seventies. In northern Myanmar, the organization reemerged as the armed division of the Shan State Progress Party; in the south, the Shan State Army is associated with a separate organization entirely, serving as the armed wing of the Restoration Council of the Shan State. A 2012 treaty with the national government granted them roles as village heads in the southern districts, granted them access to border areas and trading offices, and established them as an ally in ostensibly cooperative efforts to battle drug trafficking. In reality, things get more complicated. There are stories of child soldiers offered heroin as a part of conscription. Shan State is one of the world's leading producers of opium, and divisions of the SSA have been known to control trafficking for their own gain. "Myopic" portrays a band of child soldiers who associate themselves with the Loi Tai Leng base on the Thai border, which brushes up against the Pang Mapha District where the caverns of Tham Lot are located.

JM: Of course, most readers don't come to the story knowing any of this, so by default they're being dropped into a scene they're unfamiliar with. The politics, the culture, the slang all serve as walls that a reader may need to breach. Though the word has negative connotations not fitting of my positive usage here, I tend to use the phrase "alienating specificity" to describe stories like these—stories that don't hold the reader's hand and might even occasionally lose a reader who doesn't have Google as an aid. Breece D'J Pancake is another example that comes to mind; you'll be struggling to follow a conversation because it's so drenched in Southern slang. What do you make of this idea of "alienating specificity"? Is the risk of losing the reader's full understanding one worth considering?

MB: I like your term, and it describes one of my own central interests as a writer and reader of fiction: how does a story written in a close perspective honor its characters' consciousness without losing the reader? I think writing that relies too heavily on exposition can also alienate the reader from its characters, calling at tention to an authorial presence that's working around a limited POV. I'm in Mark Winegardner's workshop at FSU, and we're talking a lot about occasioning internality: that is, is the writing realistically portraying what the character, in this moment, would be thinking? The history of the Shan is something Gower already knows, like the Aussie slang and Thai language, so any expository description would have risked violating his POV. At Irvine, Michelle Latiolais taught me to imbed 'definitions' in context clues, providing a description or action that indicates meaning. That's what I hope that the gestural accompaniments to Phil's dialogue are accomplishing, establishing a 'key' to uncode phrases like *strewth*. The definitions of Thai felt a little more risky, but necessary. I tried to negotiate this by mobilizing Gower's translations—when he thinks of the word for cave, it's because of the way he encounters the entrance; when he defines the Thai idiom that Phil uses it's because it betrays a facility with the language that Gower hadn't expected of the Aussie. As for the historical/contextual tensions with the Shan, I tried only to convey the aspects of their history that were necessary to the immediate interpersonal tensions of the story. I was more interested in portraying the consequences of those tensions as they manifested in real individuals—Sadie losing her parents to the conflict; Aak losing his father; the child sergeant conscripted from a probable boarding school, leading his underequipped squad to track down the heroin; the Aussie running from them; and of course Gower, who is tangled up between all of these people even as he feels himself a perpetual *meung*. I think a story is always more compelling when the stakes are experienced rather than explained. The writing that is most compelling to me spends more time investigating the *how* than the *what* or the *why*. In my eyes, fiction can be an outlet to investigate the ways individuals cope with the difficult, uncomfortable, or inarticulable without the burden of providing an answer or thesis.

JM: I think you came at this from entirely the right perspective: allow the reader to learn from context without holding their hand via more direct forms of exposition, and trim for concision of exposition at every chance. Is it always necessary to include the context clues you've mentioned? What happens when there's no way to include enough context to fill the reader in? Do you cut the specificity to keep the reader, allow for more direct exposition, or honor the character by including the specificity at the reader's probable expense? You have some great examples above of instances where you found a way to fill the reader in with context, but surely every ounce of specificity to a culture or slang can't be filled in by contextual clues.

MB: I think that the short story as a form necessitates exclusion. When I'm making decisions about what background to preserve in a draft, I try to determine how that information clarifies or enhances the stakes for the main characters; if it doesn't contribute to that tension, then I cut it, perhaps at the risk of leaving the reader feeling unmoored. I hope that any dislocation this costs the story is made up for by the escalating urgency. I only try to turn to exposition when cultural details are essential to the story's tension, but I always work to occasion them as viable moments of reflection for my characters—like when Gower's looking at the map with Aak, contextualizing the fires with respect to the smugglers trying to sneak past the Shan. Of course there are going to be aspects of slang or etiquette that the story doesn't capture, but I also don't write or read fiction with the expectation of receiving a historical or anthropological account of something. If I tried for that scope in a short story I suspect it would come at the expense of narrative and character. The same goes for longer works, though perhaps less blatantly. It's something at the forefront of my mind right now as I'm revising my novel *The Needing*, trying to suss out which aspects of the characters' tangled family folklore are essential to the tension in the present and which are best left off the page.

JM: As you suggest, nailing down the exact necessary amount of exposition is a bit of a balancing game, though I think it's useful for readers to hear that you determine it all based off "tension."

"Myopic" seems to work with a sort of thematic umbrella: beyondness, going deep, blindness, escaping, leaving, etc. All of these ideas are akin to one another, operating under the same theme. What work goes into making a story so thematically cohesive, and how do these themes relate to your own life? That is to ask, what makes these ideas worth following for you personally?

MB: Janet Fitch says a novel needs to be obsessed with something, and I think this is even more true for a short story. For me, those obsessions always emerge from following characters' preoccupations. I try never to think of theme when I'm writing, but rather to follow the ideas or pressures that are urgent to characters. The concepts you bring up are all things Gower and Sadie are consumed by rather than ideas I was trying to impose on the writing. Any cohesiveness that emerges comes from an effort to inhabit their experiences.

I suppose that immersion is central to the writing process to me, and that might be part of why Gower's mind was so compelling to try and portray. Maybe his interest in "going deep" belies his own latent authorial urges.

JM: Certainly this makes sense—especially that you're not writing to theme but that it emerges naturally because the characters are fully formed and cohesive—but by the same token, you've invented Gower and Sadie. Something about their personalities, their desires took hold of you and helped you create them, no? Do their themes link up at all with your personal life? If Fitch says a novel needs to be obsessed with something, this ends up being true of the author, too.

MB: Maybe the writing process itself is an act of obsession. We immerse ourselves in the world of our characters, and by occupying their preoccupations we take on those preoccupations, too. Gower and Sadie may have emerged from my own interest in testing edges. Before I was writing seriously, I was racing triathlons and running one-hundred miles a week. Physical exhaustion alters perception just as effectively as Gower's immersion in the cave or the mushroom shakes at the full moon parties Sadie longs to sneak off to. All of these states dissolve sensory borders. In a more literal sense, I'm drawn to the same kind of immersive travel that Gower craves: relocating somewhere totally foreign to me and getting to know it closely, becoming fluent, taking root.

JM: All *Driftwood* fiction goes through several rounds of comprehensive line-edits. We believe in polishing our fiction to its utmost potential. Could you talk a bit about the process of working through revisions with *Driftwood Press*? What changes happened, and why?

MB: This has been my first opportunity to work on a story with an editor, and I worry that it's spoiled me. Our exchange helped me identify blindspots in my style that were inhibiting clarity in the story on the level of structure as well as the line. Our revisions addressed places where figuration and syntax were confusing, where a lack of description obscured the point of entry into scene, and where the logic of characters' choices wasn't apparent enough to achieve verisimilitude. We worked most on the rhythm and register of the opening paragraph, which in my initial draft leaned a bit too academic to jive with the rest of Gower's internality, and on the plotting that gestured toward Sadie's choice to take heroin in the final scene. Our exchanges resulted in dialogue that signals her potential interest in the drug during her barside conversation with Phil, and in a more explicit account of Gower's 'reseeing' of her in the throne room. I'm grateful to you for your careful eye, and I wish that this level of exchange was a more common practice among literary magazines.

JM: I wish it was, too. Most magazine editors either don't have the time or don't think it's proper to help edit another's work when there's a power dynamic present: "I'm publishing you, so you'll end up caving to what I want." Of course, the simple solution is making the recommended changes optional, as we do here at *Driftwood*; this way there's no—or at least very minimal—overstepping, and everyone benefits. I think many young writers, too, have in their mind Gordon Lish or Emily Dickinson's editor—editors who take total authorial control over the writer's work. To my mind, this is a poor editor; we do our best here at *Driftwood* to avoid overstepping and make sure the writer is prouder of the final draft than the initial—and doesn't regret any changes.

Speaking of changes, was there anything in your original conception of the story that did not make it in? Before it landed in our queue, what different forms did the story take in its three-year history?

MB: Gosh, there's been so much material between here and the first draft of this story that I'm sure there are plenty of differences that are entirely lost to me.

In its initial stages Aak and the locals were less present, but in subsequent drafts it became clear that his character played an important enough role in Gower's life—and the events of this story—that his own arc (his anxieties and suspicions over the wildfires, the loss of his father to the Shan) deserved substantive space on the page. Phil originally came across as even brasher in earlier drafts, but I worried that his portrayal leaned into the hyperbolic. Gower's backstory stretched back too far, accounting for the circumstances of his departure from his hometown for that "galactic walkabout" that had led him to Sadie. In later drafts it seemed that this exposition was less functional, as it didn't inform the present stakes of the story to the same degree as the tensions in his more recent past—those as a *meung* living with Oli, Rach, and Sadie.

JM: I noted Breece D'J Pancake above as sharing the specificity of diction. Do you think of yourself as belonging to any particular tradition? If so, who are your masters and who are your contemporaries?

MB: The writers who most inspire and excite me tend to mint their own language. Cormac McCarthy, Kevin Barry, Don Delillo, William Faulkner, Michelle Latiolais, and Kate Braverman all make so much happen in a sentence, or even a clause—both plot-wise and sensorily. They use precise, inventive diction to make sentences dense with meaning and image. That compression creates a vivid world for readers to inhabit. Latiolais's *Widow* has become a manual on fully-inhabited internality for me. I've read *Night Boat to Tangier* ten times this year, and continue to freak out over the novel's balance of scope and specificity. Maybe one necessitates the other; much of the most propulsive writing covers years with compilations of images, moments, and gestures that are gathered almost mosaically. We get the entire trajectory of Charlie's and Maurice's careers contained in the frame of their wait at the ferry terminal.

JM: Outside of what we've already discussed above, talk to me about the technical elements—the how—of minting your own language in "Myopic." I think you're following in the footsteps of these writers well—writers who, I always say, *teach you how to read them.* I'd like to hear more about how this is done—in *your* words. Feel free to grab a sentence or paragraph from "Myopic" to show us the craft decisions going into the diction.

MB: I think the stakes are highest for this kind of work in the opening of a story. Language is the point of entry for the world of the narrative, so any 'guidelines' must be established from the outset. I hope that the first paragraphs of "Myopic" work like a kind of figurative syllogism—first with the transformation of the cave, and then with Gower's transformation of senses when he enters that space in the initial two paragraphs.

Your edits on this passage were particularly productive for the story. We trimmed the sentences down to compounding figurations which bleed into Gower's actual sensory experience of the cave. The story's concrete world is 'minted' out of metaphorical language, rather than vice versa. Maybe this gives the reader rootedness in Gower's perspective by signaling that his perceptions are the lens through which they view this story? Since we're seeing through his eyes, 'concrete' details are no more stable than figuration.

JM: What other mediums have influenced your work? How? The Thai filmmaker Apichatpong Weerasethakul comes to mind, but other than him I'm woefully uninformed about Thai art. Did you plunge into Thai art, film, or fiction at all while researching?

MB: Yes! I've been obsessed with Weerasethakul ever since I stumbled into a screening of *Uncle Boonmee* as an undergraduate. I admire how his plotlines leave the viewer room to intuit, and find it instructive. His camerawork and curation of image might be another example of your term 'alienating specificity.' I studied art history as an undergraduate, and all visual forms of narrative have always interested me (and, by extension, my characters). The mammoth-bison image that Phil describes is nonfictional; it was discovered at the prehistoric settlement of Font-de-Gaume, and is generally agreed to be the earliest known example of an optical illusion. Our modern incarnation of the image would be the duck-rabbit. I think the image's 'trick' is something I value in fiction: a narrative that first signals one thing, but upon closer examination leads the reader toward another; yet when we cast back, we recognize what we were looking at the whole time. I'm thinking about stories like Edward P. Jones's "Lost in the City," Alice Munro's "Corrie," and George Saunders's "Bohemians."

JM: A few days from now, after "Myopic" has sat in the reader's gut and gestated, what do you want the reader to realize it was signaling? What's the "trick"?

MB: I think that the biggest wound Gower sustains in this story is his own recognition that he's never really understood Sadie. He'll never fully know her, this cave, or this culture, nor would she ever have known him. He's kept his own secrets from her. He'd found her parents' bodies in the bottom of the cave years before, but never told her because he'd thought that she was sticking around in the hope that they'd return. When he finds Sadie in the throne room, he believes that she was never waiting for them in the first place, but for the heroin smugglers. I think Gower's recognition that he's misread her motives is the real hurt he crawls away from in the end.

JM: I'll be curious and hopeful to hear how much of that comes through to the first-time reader. So much of your paragraph above is so expertly boiled down to a single sentence that appears after the mine lights: "He'll always be *meung* to her."

I'm sure readers will read "Myopic" and be desperate to read more of Mason Boyles. Do you have any other publications available for readers to get their hands on?

MB: I've been working on novels for the past two years; the last story I published, "Liminal," appeared in the *Wisconsin Review* in early 2019. Right now, I'm seeking representation for my novel *Bark On*, which follows two triathletes preparing for an Ironman in a flooding beach town that's combatting a rising population of coyotes. There's folk magic, superstition, and painkillers. I also have some new stories I've workshopped at FSU this fall, so I hope that those and the novel will be out in the world soon.

JM: You've mentioned your novel *The Needing* a few times in this interview. We know it features a good bit of family history, coal mining, and the development of North Carolinian highways, but you never told us the premise.

MB: *The Needing*, a family saga following the youngest heirs to a failing coal dynasty. Twins Fish and Laz Locklear are living in Hurrah, North Carolina, under the shadow of their family's convoluted history. They live with their Ma and uncle Orby in their grandparents' mansion. Orby and Ma brew moonshine in an attempt to recreate their grandparents' memory-erasing recipe. When the two lose cahoots, Orby aims his wrath at the twins, and a familiar stranger helps them escape to the flooded beach town of Galore. There Laz and Fish discover another side of their family history—and a way to escape it. But Laz believes he's bound to the land that his grandparents mined by a generational curse described to them by Orby. Fish must choose whether to leave his twin behind or try to free him from the violence that Laz believes to be his destiny. The novel investigates the way that abuse, addiction, and ecological damage obscure a community's relationship with its history, and how that blurring can perpetuate abuse. I think that the protagonists in both projects—*Bark On* and *The Needing*—rely on superstition as an etiquette for their compulsions.

JM: Interesting! I'll be excited to buy either book when it finds a publisher! Is there anything you'd like to say as we close out this interview? Any parting words for our readers?

MB: Thanks, James, and thanks to everyone at *Driftwood Press*. There's an enormous amount of labor that goes into getting a literary magazine together, especially one that's so aesthetically pleasing. I'm excited to have my work appear alongside other great writers as well as visual artists. The illustrations, poems, and stories are all put into dialogue, and the website and print edition are both beautiful. I hope that readers enjoy the work in this issue with an appreciation for the effort that went into its creation and curation. It continues to baffle me that anyone takes the time out of their day to give an eye to my work, and I'm abundantly grateful to them for doing it. Please keep supporting literary magazines! It's the best way to keep great writing showing up in our mailboxes.

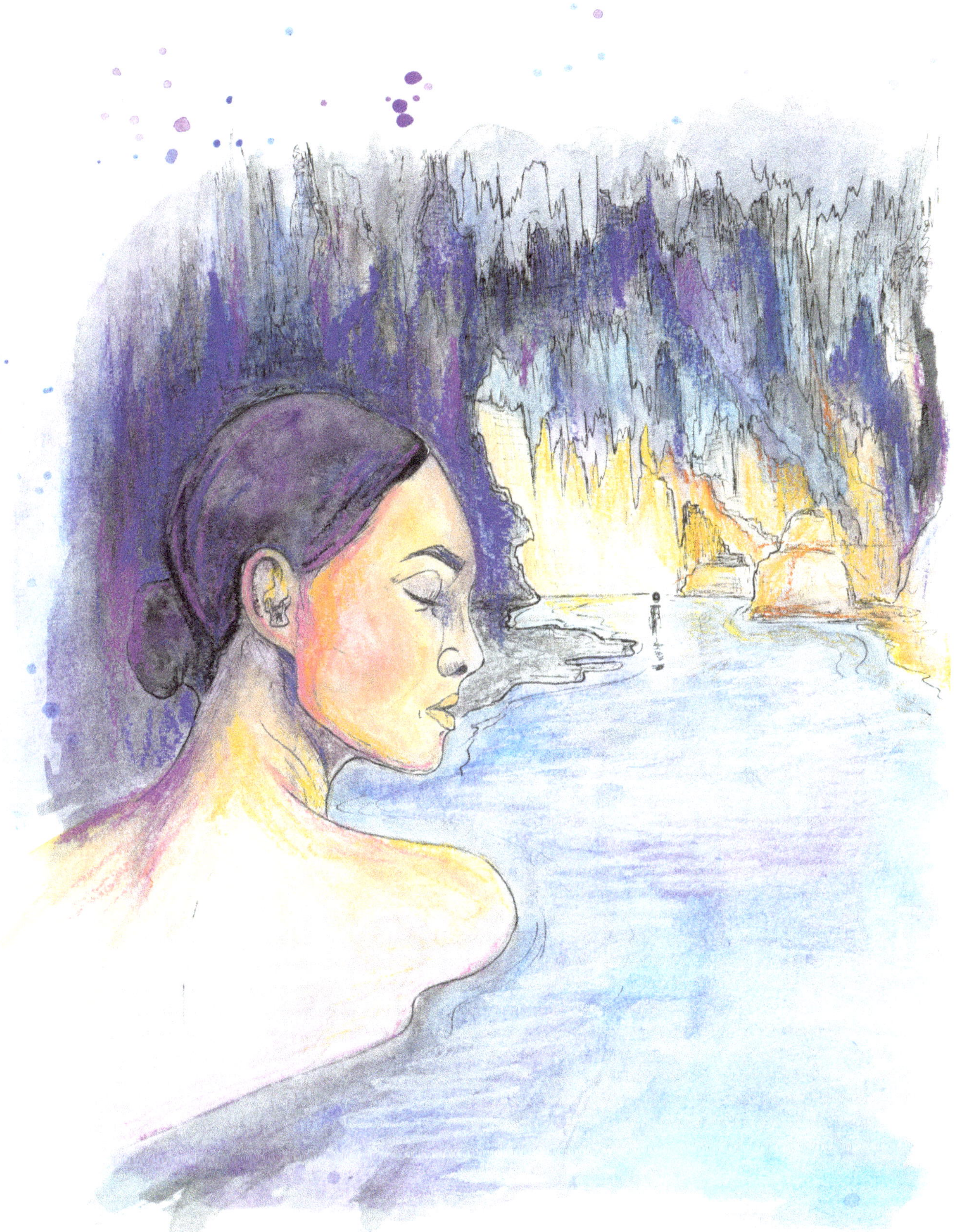

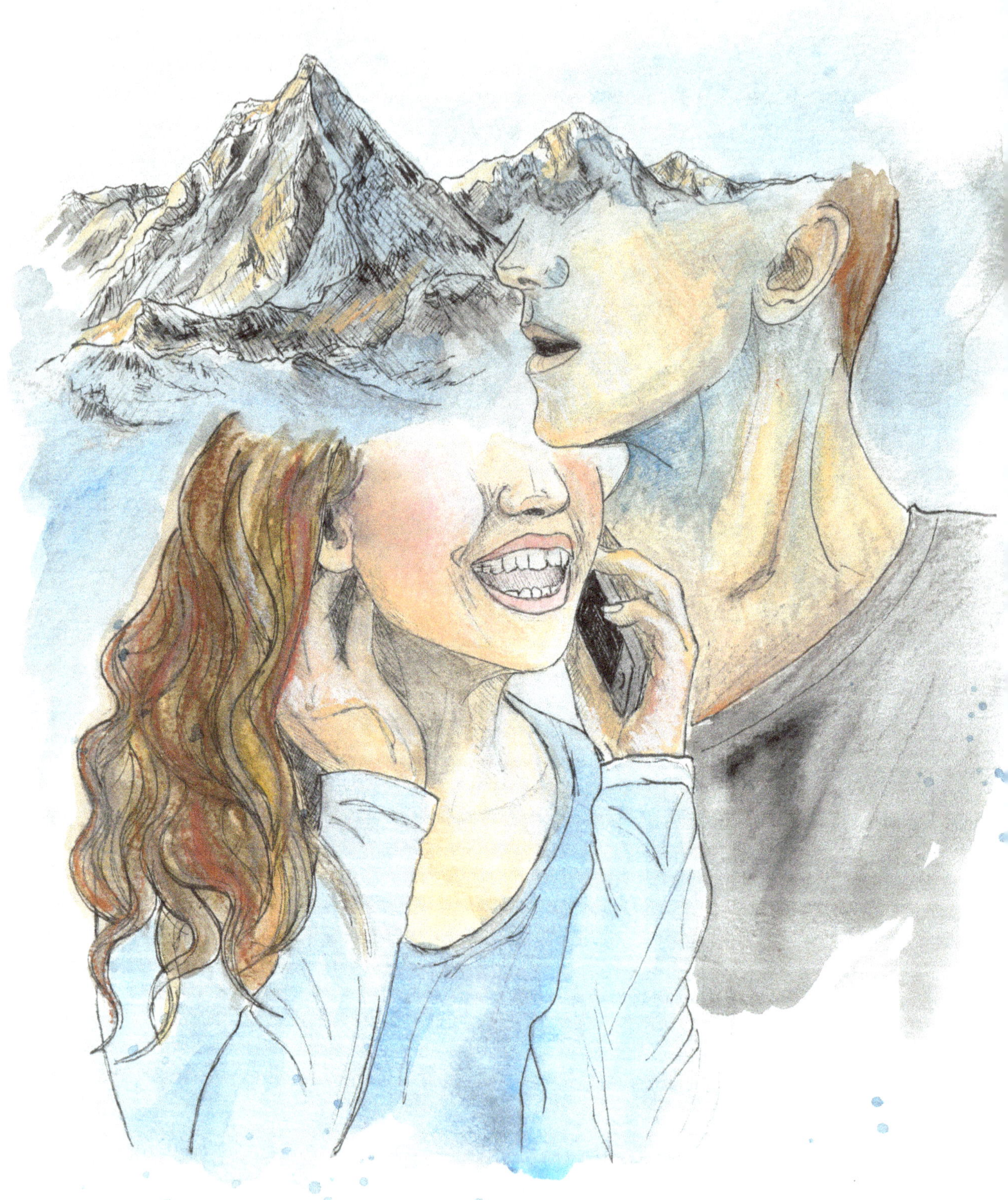

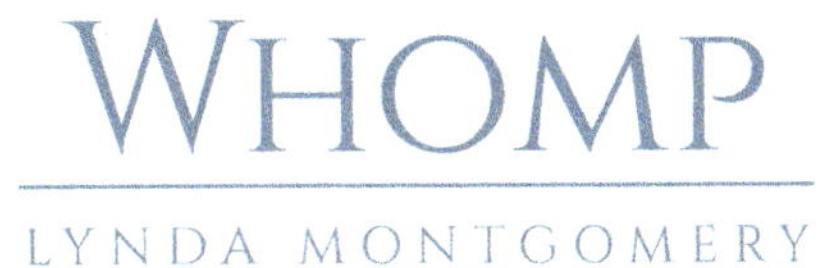

Whomp

LYNDA MONTGOMERY

Today, the fourth day after the avalanche, I get up to my alarm, shower, shave, and drive thirty-five miles to work at Specialty One, western Montana's top provider of online and telephonic support for Comcast and other national brands. They called the search off after two days. The boss said *take as long as you need*, but I didn't need long. Being a diligent younger brother, as always, I spent three days calling our relatives and opening Aidan's door to neighbors with food. The whole time I was drunk or hungover or in that middle ground where it's both.

I head to my workspace on the far side of the room. A few older women stop to hug me, but the younger ones and guys stick with eye contact and nonverbal gestures, the chin-up *hey* mostly. My cube, undecorated and empty except for the mug that my ex-girlfriend Nikki gave me, looks no different. A cloud of burrito smell passes through—the ghost of coworker Dave's every meal. I spend more time than usual adjusting the height of my chair and fiddling with my headset while my workstation powers up.

"You're on a recorded line for quality assurance. My name is Logan. Good morning, and how can I help you?" The script that scrolls on my screen changes the greeting—*morning, afternoon, evening*—according to the time zone of the incoming call. I wonder how often that gets messed up now that people have moved all over but kept their same numbers, but no one has told me—even at the advanced training.

My first caller says, "My WiFi cut out and don't tell me to fucking unplug everything."

A man's voice, probably, with an accent that matches the Wisconsin area code. "I've already spent a half hour crawling around unplugging and re-plugging and it hadn't done shit."

I follow the script. "So, you're having trouble with your internet. Do you also have a landline phone?" Outside my window, a few deer and their shadows move through the woods behind the parking lot. The juvenile rough-legged hawk perches on his usual branch near the top of a dead Ponderosa pine.

"No, and don't tell me to..."

I tune out the rest. He is what Burrito Dave calls a long-vent—it's not an official caller category. I mute the line and pull up his audio waveform and start another call, from Texas. Dave taught me the hack—without listening we can see when folks peter out—it's been a boon for increasing my calls per hour.

The Texas call is a direct send-up, or DS, which is an official caller category. Us long-termers take them in rotation so everyone's numbers suffer equally if a DS takes too long to clear. DSs get that label by calling three times within twenty-four hours, pressing *zero* numerous times in quick succession, or yelling agent at such volume and pitch that the computer's analysis deems an 85% likelihood they will complain on multiple social media platforms.

An automated introduction plays before my microphone opens... *Based in the United States with at least six months' experience, we guarantee that our Gold-level representative will handle your concern satisfactorily 95% of the time...*

Most of us hate DSs, preferring instead the worn-out seething of someone who has been on hold for twenty minutes. Regular people clear quickly because they want to shower or have sex or do whatever you don't usually do while on an assistance call with Specialty One. A little dump, jerk-off, or changing the bandage on their uncle's amputation are all fair game for surviving phone holds, I have, unfortunately, learned from experience.

Wisconsin continues to ramble, but I cut him off with, "May I place you on a brief hold?" On another line, I introduce myself to the DS, Lia, and start the call report log.

"I need to pay bills and I can't get online with the bank and I have been stuck at home with a puking toddler and I am starting to heave in the back of my throat so I really don't…"

"Might I suggest Gatorade and popsicles?"

"That's not funny." She sounds young and, I'm guessing, not a native Texan, because she speaks like a newscaster even though she's mad as hell.

At last month's conference call, I told them that the humor-opening performed poorly on DSs, but corporate insisted on that step and you never could tell when they were monitoring.

I reply using my own line. "Let's start with what you've tried."

"Rebooted modem and computer. Checked the connections, looked at the wires coming into my house, consulted with neighbors about a wider outage. I have a PhD in engineering, which is why I am super mad."

She burps halfway through the last sentence—a long, wet cowboy belch.

"I can imagine."

I gain access to her account and run tests according to the *nonspecific outage protocol.* The Wisconsin long-vent demands a supervisor, so I pass him up. When I ping Lia's modem everything runs fine and I tell her.

"Great," she says. "It's always like that. Same with the kids. They'll be sick as dogs for a week and when I finally take them in, they're bouncing off the walls and the nurse gives me that look."

"The *don't waste my time or you poor thing*?" These questions aren't part of the scripts, but I find that a little conversation helps keep my caller-satisfaction numbers up.

"Poor thing but with genuine sympathy. I must give off unskilled mother vibes."

I roll the chair back from the desk and scan the office—cubicle walls, ceiling tile, and Dave's Birkenstocked feet sticking into the aisle. "I've been getting that look all day."

"Why?" she asks.

"My brother died in an avalanche four days ago and I watched the whole thing."

An alert pops up: *Your call with [LIA from AMARILLO, TX] shows no log note or actions for that last thirty seconds. Remember to update your call log or give a proper sign-off and close the call.*

"Are you serious?"

"Yep. It's real. We're backcountry skiers. In Montana."

"What happened?" she asks, and on her side of the line a trill of small voices follows. She tells them to hang on. "Oh, God. Forgive me. You don't have to say anything."

I can't say anything because suddenly I forget my story. I close my eyes, flip my mic up, and put my head on the desk. After a beat, I recover, tip back in the chair. "Avalanches are like lotteries. That's what Aidan, my brother, always said."

"But that doesn't make it any less tragic," Lia says. "How are you doing?"

Her question is genuine. In my mind, she looks like Nikki's sister—if Nikki had one. Not nerdy and not undone by motherhood.

"I shouldn't be talking to you about this," I answer. My computer screen fills with pop-ups, and now there's a blipping in my left earphone.

"It's all right. Puts my WiFi troubles in perspective."

"They haven't found him yet." I swallow hard. "His body."

A voiceover breaks into my line. *Thanks for giving Gold-level service. This call is now being automatically forwarded.*

And she is gone. Outside, the hawk alights and the recoil of the tree triggers an isolated snow shower. I close the call log but the damage to my metrics has been done—*REFERRED TO CENTRAL*—pasted in the final disposition box. I tear off my headset and stare at the screen until the image blurs. I roll my chair back from the workstation and melt—a slow cascade until I am lying on the floor. One of the screws holding the seat of my chair to its base has threaded itself nearly out and above the grid of ceiling tiles oscillates in and out of focus. The smell of carpet cleaner and dust fills my nose, and a migraine blooms behind my eyes.

***

That day we took our usual route, snowmobiling halfway up Swan's Neck from the trailhead, then trekking the rest. All was quiet except for the distant chainsaw buzz of snowmobiles and the crunch of our boots, Aidan's right landing flat and loud because of his bad knee. Despite the cloud cover and keeping all my jacket vents open, I was sweaty ten minutes into the hike. The entire cycle—heart-thumping, steady walking for two hours followed by twenty minutes of speed, quick turns, frigid air forcing itself back into the deepest regions of your chest, all in the wide alone—that's backcountry. Low landers who ride lifts and stay inbounds could never understand. Neither Aidan nor I wasted breath trying to convince them.

***

On day nine, they find Aidan using cadaver dogs. Someone from Mountain Rescue says he probably died in the slide and not after, but they don't say how they know. The Funeral Director says nothing and I wonder whether, instead, it was clear from the body that Aidan suffocated after several clearheaded minutes with the realization that no one was digging for him.

Aidan was single, having divorced wife number two a year ago. Since our parents are long gone, as next-of-kin, I have to deal with both the legal stuff and the stuff-stuff. Everyone focuses on the emotional aspects of grief and leaves out how much of a pain in the ass death is. Until I have the death certificate I can't do any paperwork, but I hold on to Aidan's phone and cancel with anyone who calls to follow-up on bidded work. Aidan's main guy, Toby, moves ahead with ongoing projects and, in exchange, I offer him either Aidan's truck and tools or the balance from the finished jobs. Toby chooses the dough. Aidan's landlady was real nice and gave me a month free, so I didn't have to clear out right away.

I am in his place now, two and a half weeks after, wishing I had the guts to call Nikki or somebody to help. I think of poor Aunt Pat. She'd called us a few times eighteen years ago, when we were back in Kalispell shortly after our parents' funeral, asking when we were returning to help. They went two at once. The rented preacher, who knew nothing of my drunk driving father and codependent mother, repeated the phrase throughout the bland service, and everyone seemed to pick up on it, repeating their sympathies for our two-at-once losses with their coffee-breath hugs. Aidan and I never answered Aunt Pat, and she simply took care of everything. Six months after their accident, and four months after the big checks that would solidify our ability to live the ski bum life for a little longer, a few boxes arrived. Last week she mailed a sympathy card to me in care of Aidan's ex, with a note inside saying that it was the only address she had.

I pound back a third shot, crank my tunes, and open Aidan's bedroom door. The smell stops me—like evergreens after a heavy snowstorm. My mind is playing tricks, but it doesn't matter, it puts me back on the mountain.

Someone had stripped the bed and took away the old dresser. Like all of his furniture, the dresser hadn't been acquired so much as landed there and got put to use. His animals were all like that, too. Somebody distributed them that first week, so I wouldn't have to worry. I was fine with parting ways with the cats, goat, and his lesser dog.

His good dog, Pepper, went to his ex-wife, and the two of them show up as I haul the last few loads to my car. I bend down to get my face full of the mutt's love. His silky ears almost make me forget who I am.

"I didn't say anything at the memorial." She always starts like this. I like her, more now after they split, but she has a bad habit of turning up unannounced and then making you feel like the one imposing. I lean against the stair rail of the porch. She sits on the other one.

"You can have whatever you like," I say.

"Oh. Not that." She reaches into her jacket pocket and throws a tennis-ball-on-rope across the yard. "It's Aidan. His ashes. He wanted me to have them."

"He never said anything about it." Pepper brings the toy back to me and I huck it nearly to the woods' edge.

"Maybe. But he said it to me. More than once. I have something I need to do with them. I owe it to him."

"You don't owe him anything. Not for a long time," I say, keeping my gaze directed at Pepper.

"Don't be like that."

"You know he didn't leave a will," I say.

"I bet he told Toby." She pulls out her phone.

"Leave Toby alone," I say, but I never want to argue. The booze has worn off and I feel the back of my neck go tight. "There's a crypt back in California, where my parents…"

"You know Aidan wouldn't like being stuck near a strip mall in Fresno."

"I might go back up Swan's Neck with them. In summer."

She starts opening doors of my old Accord. "They're in here, right?"

On her second dive, she comes out with a shopping bag stamped *Mountain Eternity*, weighted by what they call a cardboard urn but is really just a twenty-five-dollar box that I haven't been able to look at since the Funeral Director handed it over. She sets it on the step and lifts the lid. Inside there's a thick plastic bag closed with a long twist tie.

"It's your word against mine," she says. "So we should just split them. Got a trash bag?" She's already working the ties.

"I don't know…"

"You were with him. You got a chance to say good-bye, Logan. Want to know the last thing he said to me? Nothing."

Pepper returns and I grab his collar, but he's pulling toward the box and we all start yelling. I haven't found a bag and she's screaming at me and the dog but doesn't quit untwisting the tie. Before I can say something that will change her mind or slow her down, she reaches for a five-gallon bucket, dumps out the few cans and bottles that Aidan put there for recycling, and pours in half of the gray sand that was my brother. A cloud lifts. Pepper and I both lean our heads over and sniff.

***

When we reached the summit that day, Aidan performed his ritual, communing with our Lord, and only I knew a hint of sincerity was involved. He stood tall, raised his arms wide, yelled, "Thanks, Fucker!" and, sometimes, pissed his initials in the snow. I don't remember if he peed that day.

We started the descent slowly. As always, sometimes I would lead and sometimes he would. Ideally, we kept a line of sight after the first open face, but, because of the glades, it wasn't always possible. But I could hear him. We tagged up for a second near the edge of a small lake. Our usual route was to traverse east for the best entry to a bowl midway down.

"These goggles are for shit," he said, and pushed off.

***

I notice how dusk comes later, and when we have a bright day the parking lot outside my office window gets crisscrossed by dark rivulets of snowmelt draining away from the plowed-up mounds. Someone sawed down the hawk's dead pine tree and left the logs stacked in a neat pile at the edge of the woods. During the last hour of my shift one Wednesday, a month after the avalanche, I get another DS from Lia with a note: *request Logan if available.* I have never been requested before and reading the call screen makes my stomach drop.

Her voice is bright. "The WiFi again. I'm beginning to think it's gremlins."

"Let me pull up my gremlin protocol."

She laughs at the humor opening this time. I picture her tucking a loose strand of hair behind her ear.

I start the diagnostics and type a line into the call report. Glad she called but not sure what to do, I choose a script: *Small Talk Option A.* "How's the weather in Amarillo?"

"Oh. I am not in Amarillo anymore. We moved to Fort Collins, Colorado last year."

"Gotcha." I update her about the systems tests and there's a pause. I debate telling her about what happened with Aidan's ex, but she pipes up before I figure out what to say.

"Colorado's terrific, beautiful, but far from my in-laws and all of our friends. My husband's new job has him traveling all the time."

"Sounds lonely."

"Maybe that's why I called," she says.

My ear hums and a tingle runs through my jaw and throat.

"The four-part Gold Star analysis has unfortunately not identified a reason for your repeated signal drop. May I put you on a brief hold?"

I transfer the official conversation from phone to online chat and then dial her back from my cell phone. "I don't want big brother to cut us off this time."

I hear her sigh.

On chat, she and I correspond about her WiFi and, on the phone, she tells me about her life. Like a game of footsy at Thanksgiving dinner. Her two sons are young, rambunctious, and sick all the time. She loves her husband but feels he pressured her into the move. She lost her friends and can't muster the energy to look for a job. As she tells me her story, I google and find a picture from four years ago—the graduate engineering program at West Texas A&M. She has lighter features than Nikki and wears less makeup, too.

"I kept thinking about your brother," she says. "And you. I couldn't stop thinking about what you must have gone through."

"Yeah."

"Do you think about it?"

"Constantly." There's silence while I wait for her to say something that will heal me, but she doesn't. "People keep trying to taking me skiing…"

"That's fucked up." She whispers the line, and I remember that her children must be right there. She hasn't described them in detail, but I picture them—they resemble her husband, also imagined, only with round cheeks and square-banged haircuts. The older one walks around wearing one sock, and the little one has crumbs plastered in the corners of his mouth.

"I do need to break the association at some point. I might need till next year." I have five other chats going and three flash red because it's been over twenty seconds since I've typed something. I use keystroke commands to issue *Delay Apology 2A* in all of them, including hers. On the phone, I tease another story from her. Running through my mind is a conversation between Aidan and me. I can see us, walking with Pepper along Flathead Lake. His week's-worth of stubble is half gray. *Like everything, you have two options*, he says in the daydream. "Take action or stand there like a dumbass," I finish Aidan's line.

"What?" Lia asks.

"Sorry, that was something Aidan, my brother, said."

"Everybody thinks engineers love those simple binaries, but things are always more complicated."

"Most people think I pussied out. That my surviving is evidence of cowardly behavior."

"Everything okay?" Burrito Dave leans in my cubicle, holding the namesake food. A small drizzle of cheese hangs, like a spider rappelling on her silk, threatening the upholstered mini-wall that shelters me. My screen is a hot mess.

"Gotta go." I say to Lia and hang up. I type the command for *Medium Hold Permission* across all chats.

"Need me to run a little interference with the boss? I'm good with that kind of thing, now," Dave says.

"Now?" I ask. Giving Dave my full attention is the best way to get rid of him.

"My girlfriend dragged me to a relationship skills workshop. That shit works wonders around here."

"No kidding," I say.

"Not that you asked, but I'd be careful. Griffin is still cutting you slack, but he can't do much if your metrics tank for more than a couple weeks." He took a small bite and kept talking. "I've seen it a few times. They let old Marcy go before she was halfway through her chemo."

Somewhere after Bozeman, half-moon sitting on the foothills that hug the road, the tire pressure signal lights up a moment before the car pulls and thumps. I make it to the shoulder with only one asshole blaring his horn as he swerves and blows past. In the trunk, half of Aidan in the five-gallon bucket blocks access to the spare. I set it on the gravel behind me but only for a second before I picture myself accidentally kicking it over. I secure the bucket in the footwell of back passenger side and replace the piece of cardboard serving as lid.

Lying on the icy road, fingers already numb and scraped from trying to get the jack in place, I hear Aunt Pat.

"Try a little harder not to take after your father," she says.

"That's Aidan." I say, out loud, and hear him yell, "Fuck that!"

Aidan had no time for family resemblance talk, and in this way, he was exactly like our father. My allegiances to family and home were always more complicated. I can't draw the line directly, but something about all of it and Lia's call led me to skip the turnoff for home after my shift and continue on 83. When I stopped to pee and get coffee after a hundred miles, I committed fully—opened up the picture I had taken of Lia's information from my workstation screen and plugged *2874 Aruba Lane, Fort Collins* into Maps. I will get there by morning.

My right side has frozen to prickles. I tighten the lug nuts, release the jack, put everything away, then do twenty jumping jacks to get the blood going before driving again. This whole episode is where most people would snap to their senses and limp back home. I picture Burrito Dave, inside a warm house, not using his new relationship skills properly.

I made the sensible choice once.

Aidan and I knew the possibilities. We had always known them, even before the funerals. *He died as he lived* and all that crap. I can't say whether our past made us any more reckless than others, but everyone craves reasons. Our crowd could repeat the standard ones—youth, testosterone, an underdeveloped frontal cortex, or a broken heart. Some got philosophical and said shit like, *he wasn't tough enough to get old.* True that it took a certain hardness to be one of those ancient cowboys with their oxygen and wheelchairs, every part of them shrunken. The only reminders of who they had been were their hats and the occasional zinger you'd catch if you could understand what the hell they were saying.

Aidan would have said something stupid like it was *a damn fine day to die* without considering whether that could ever be true. He came late to skiing with a helmet and rode his Kawasaki without one, saying he'd rather go out boldly and donate his black heart to someone else than end up broken in all the other ways. We'd known guys like that, too. Instead of wakes, we had been to the parties—*He's fucked up for the rest of his life, but he got fucked up as he lived.* It didn't have the same ring, and the gatherings were dreadful.

Living in Montana teaches you about space and scale. It takes a few years for Californians to figure out that the four-hour drive to Helena is nothing; folks from back east usually leave before they ever get close. Cruising through the night, full speed on the spare, I learn that the high plains of Wyoming are one step further—darkness makes you feel like you are inside a planetarium, though with the occasional intrusion of manmade light. In college, I learned that intermittent reinforcement is the most addicting; it's how slot machines work, and being out here is the same—the randomly spaced lights from a house, barn, or warehouse tug at my soul. I hope Lia still looks like her grad school picture. She's cute, but I prefer the imperfections—her crooked smile and the thin scar on the bridge of her nose.

A few hours after the flat, lighted signs report a slowdown, I'm on 90, south of the Crow reservation and there aren't any other routes southeast. The trucks and I track together, a ribbon of red lights, at thirty-two miles an hour. I fuss with the music—first hip hop, then roots rock, but then Aidan's in my ear telling me to shut that twangy shit down. I look over my shoulder, tell the bucket to go to hell and turn the volume up. Almost midnight and I am hungry.

In the gas station bathroom, a voice talks at me from over the sink. Not Aidan, thank God. More like the voice actor who does the DS intro. *You're driving through the night to woo a married woman you met on the phone…* I brush the water from my cheeks and growl at the blank wall. *In the car where half of your brother's cremains have been sitting for two weeks.*

The voice would use the word *cremains.*

I stand in front of the coolers and consider buying some wine. Not that we would drink it—I should make Lia's by nine a.m.—but maybe as a gesture. My other gift options are: silk rose, lottery ticket, a four-pack of apple BlackNMilds. I go for everything except the smokes.

The cashier rings me up without making the small talk I planned to answer with the story I'd made up about where I was going. I start to tell her anyhow, but she keeps her head in her phone. I take a step toward the door when a hand clamps hard on my shoulder.

"Sir!" A skinny old rancher in coveralls puts himself between me and the door. "You gonna pay for those?" I could take him, if it weren't for the surprise and his fetid breath.

A roar of adrenaline courses through me and the scene warps—shelves of cigarettes and lottery tickets bubble and recede like a reflection in a convex mirror. My voice stays calm. "What's going on?"

"The mugs." A few feet away stands a tower with souvenir coffee cups decorated with grandpa jokes, trucker jokes, and ones like the two he pulls from my coat pockets that read *Wyoming or Just a Rectangle*? I don't remember idly shoplifting, but he's holding up evidence.

In an instant, I drop the coffee and gifts that I paid for, duck out of my coat, and race for the door. Crouched low, action-movie style, I make it to my car and peel out. The rancher gets a few shots off, but the car and I remain untouched, so I guess he aimed into the air. I race several miles down the road, always choosing a turn when I can, then slow and stop, playing possum on a gravel road that ends where an abandoned barn slumps into the lane.

I take a few minutes to catch my breath, then follow the calm directions of the emotionless map-voice back to the interstate. A hundred miles later, the thrill of the chase wears off and leaves a knifing headache in its place. I grieve the large sugary coffee puddled on the floor of the minimart. I miss it like I miss my brother.

***

I didn't see Aidan get taken up by the slide. As we worked our way eastward, I detoured through a small glade and emerged from the trees a couple hundred yards uphill. I heard it before I could scan downhill for a skier—Aidan undoubtedly stopped and waiting to rag on me for being slow. A whomp. Followed by the cloud—an updraft of snow roiling like whitewater into the sky.

I skied hard toward Aidan's tracks, then stopped the instant the avalanche registered in thought. I couldn't feel any part of myself, everything had gone to buzzing, like I was no longer in a body. I waited to be taken up by the slide, too, to give myself over to timelessness. Under my skis, the powder settled a tiny bit. But I stood well above the slab and remained glued to the mountain.

I leaned downhill and slid a few feet. Then somebody's yelling in my ear *Stop Stop Stop*. I complied, carving my skis deep into the slope. I balled myself up, head tucked to the top of my boots, the voice now muffled from a roar of ocean surf. My vision went dark and splotchy. I ripped off my helmet and collapsed back into the snow. Icy flakes sifted on my face.

Breathe, you're here. Breathe. I sat up and planted a pole downhill as anchor. Blinked a few times before the slide came into focus. The air was filled with the metallic reek of rocks and water vapor and the sharp bite of sap from small firs busted up in the flow. It had gotten quiet much faster than I could have imagined, I realized, when I again heard a hum of distant snowmobiles.

I closed my eyes for a moment.

"You need to think." This time, I muttered aloud, the words tangled in my chapped lips.

I had twenty minutes. That's what they teach in avalanche safety. Following his path wouldn't save that much time and substantially risked triggering a second slide, plus I'd still have to find his beacon and dig him out. I calculated small chance upon smaller chance and ended up with infinitesimal. I'd do anything for him, but he didn't support futile efforts. We knew what going two at once did to people.

The realization that he was gone seemed to come from the same trampled down place as my shallow breathing. I began to traverse back east. The plume of snow mist had already begun to disperse—tiny crystals sparkling in the sunlight.

***

When eight a.m. rolls around, emails and texts from work start arriving. First, a reminder message from Central about scheduling a metrics review with my supervisor. Then, more automated ones telling me to complete a time-off form if I am a sick. Finally, a call from Burrito Dave.

"Everything okay?" On the phone, I hear traces of his Hawaii youth. "Boss asked me to call."

"Oh, hey, thanks. I'm all right. Took my friend's kid to the ER last night. Appendicitis." The lie takes me by surprise.

"I'll pass it along."

"Do you know why he asked you to call me?" I ask.

"Not really. Maybe I am the one who knows you best. And, because of what happened?"

"Oh." They have me on a tacit suicide watch. From the boss's perspective, it wasn't far-fetched to think that I might end myself—others in my situation post-avalanche had done it. Unnerving, though, to have people wonder that about you. I spend the next sixty miles picturing Dave, the boss, and the older women all talking about me.

Holding the steering wheel against the pulling spare makes my elbow tight and pinkie numb. The traffic is back, and the lady robot in my phone has a lot to say as interstates merge then twist away from each other. Soon she talks me off I-25, through an industrial park and along a main road, one of those strips flanked by national chain stores. Two turns later, I enter Stanton Creek, a subdivision marked by a faux gate made of brick. These aren't brand new homes, but not terribly old, I surmise, based on the twenty-foot trees planted at regular intervals. Before I was hired at Specialty One, I helped Aidan on houses like these in Kalispell—beveled glass windows, vaulted-ceiling atriums, and siding in one of four colors—they were already falling apart.

I flash ahead to alternate futures. Lia and I are getting married, back east wherever her family lives. Aidan has agreed to fly in, and he hates flying. Next clip, I show up back at his house, noting the recycling bucket in its old place on the porch, and tell him about this crazy trip. I don't have to embellish anything to make it a good tale. The clips get shorter and weirder and they all end with a close-up of his face.

The robot says, "In zero point three miles, you will arrive at your destination."

I pull over to review my speech. I twist to retrieve my wool cap from the back where it lay since I tossed it during the chase. The cardboard top had slipped off Aidan at some point.

Here's what I think. Everyone makes choices that are heroic or cowardly depending on their core beliefs and perspective. Most of these choices are invisible—either made in an instant or so drawn out that the actual inflection point, the beginning of the slide, is indiscernible. Unfathomable to yourself and others, at the moment, and in reflection. My choice on the mountain happened to be the rare one that showed. To me and to everyone who considers the events for more than a second. Am I enviable for being in the unique position of knowing that I made a choice? Or do I deserve pity?

I feel the cry rise up and decide to give over to it for a minute. No way can I talk to Lia if I don't.

Lia's husband opens the door for me. From behind his legs, a small child watches—I can't tell which one. But I made up so much about her kids that I don't know where her facts ended and my fantasy began. I wave my badge, making a point to aim it at the boy, too, and tell the husband that I am here for the service call his wife arranged.

"She didn't say anything. Who are you with again?"

"Specialty One. We're on contract for your wireless internet."

"Gotcha." He lets me in and points me to a small office accessed through the great room. He kicks aside a few toys that litter the route. "Sorry for the mess. The kids have been sick and…"

"Yeah, Lia told me."

"What?"

I walk quickly and hope that the kid distracts the husband away from my blunder. The office is a small room with a window that looks out to their neighbor's rusted basketball hoop and snow-beaten shrubs.

I crouch, following my flashlight's beam to a jumble of cords under the desk. "If you don't mind, I'll check around all the connections and cables inside first. The trouble is usually outside, but we always start here."

"Help yourself. Please don't let the cat out."

He doesn't hover. Faraway, I hear him speaking to the child. Under the desk, I am hit with a lingering scent of lotion. I wiggle some cords, mumble some technical gibberish, and scramble back out. The computer screen has awakened to a picture of the family in front of a Christmas tree inside a different house. She was pregnant with the second one.

Then I step out the porch door and track along the side of the house, in the narrow space between foundation plantings and the wall. The dryer vent has plastered lint to the ground in a small blast zone. I pretend to look at wires when a minivan pulls in the driveway. Lia gets out from the driver's side and I see that she is beautiful in the way I predicted—a little older and mellower than her grad school picture. Her light brown hair, which must catch highlights in summer, is pulled back in a ponytail. She tucks her glasses in the front pocket of an oversized flannel shirt and walks toward the passenger side.

"Hey!" I wave but there's really no toning down the fact that I am a strange man emerging from the shadows along her house. "It's me. Logan."

She startles and stops, leans on the minivan's hood, and squints at me.

"From the call center. I came to see if I could fix your WiFi myself."

"Oh." She wraps her arms around herself. "Wow." The sound of a dribbled basketball echoes off the houses.

I can see her working hard to compose her reply, but I start talking before she can. "It's really no problem. After work, I didn't feel like going home. I started driving, you know, to ease my mind. At some point, I realized that Ft. Collins wasn't all that far…"

She turns to look back and I follow her gaze to the other child motionless in the car seat. She waits a moment while I ramble on.

"I shouldn't have requested you. I'm sorry. I was just so worried about you," she says.

"You said you were lonely."

"Not like that."

The husband cracks open the door and leans out. "Everything all right?"

"Fine. I'll be in in a sec." She looks at me when she talks to him. Inexplicable looks pass over her face like fast-moving clouds.

I try to muster the courage to say my piece. "I know it seems odd…"

"You should go." The way she says it, I can tell she is no longer mad or scared. She gives me that same look we talked about on that first call.

"Yeah. I know. I understand completely," I say.

She reaches inside the van and unbuckles the kid.

"Please don't think I am crazy, it was a split-second decision," I say.

"I know. They all are." She leans in, hoists the sleeping child over her shoulder. A little foot, covered by red fleece sleeper pajamas, catches on her unbuttoned shirt, revealing her waist, a grey tank top over a small bulge of flesh.

INTRUSIVE GRIEF

A CONVERSATION WITH LYNDA MONTGOMERY

The following conversation was conducted by managing fiction editor James McNulty.

James McNulty: Welcome to the pages of *Driftwood*, Lynda! We're excited to have you! Most of the authors we solicit end up in our rejection pile; "Whomp" is, so far as I know, the first story by a solicited author to make it through to publication in the past four or so years. Our editor Dan Leach recommended you submit, right? How'd that come about?

Lynda Montgomery: It's great to be here! I was interested to hear that my story's path to publication is unusual for *Driftwood*, as this is the first time I've been invited to submit to a literary journal. As a dedicated slush pile submitter, I am heartened by your anecdote, even as I realize the low probability for acceptances from slush as well. Dan and I were introduced through a mutual mentor, the writer Dean Bakopoulos. Dean, being familiar with my fiction and Dan's editorial work and proclivities, thought we might make a match. Dan agreed that the story might be fit for *Driftwood*, and that's how the manuscript began to work its way through your solicited work queue. I will add that despite 'connections' being part of this story's path of publication, I do not consider myself to be a writer that is emerging from traditional literary circles. I do not have an MFA, but instead, over years of attending readings, conferences, residencies, and, more recently, through work as a reader for other publications, have developed a wider writing community, which is rewarding and helps sustain me through the lonelier aspects of our craft.

JM: We don't solicit often, but when we do, the story goes through the same process as other submissions. The stories we select tend to come from normal and contest submissions, and about half the writers we publish are early in their career. Certainly, your story makes the convincing case that you don't need an MFA to be a great writer, and I'm glad you've found another way to enter the community. Let's start by talking a little bit about the conception process for "Whomp." Tell us about its origins before it landed in our submission queue.

LM: "Whomp" began as a response to a prompt. I have mixed feelings about prompts, generally. Several years ago, I had the great fortune to take a generative workshop co-taught by Lynda Barry and Dan Chaon. We spent much of our time writing in response to images and words often chosen at random. Those exercises, and Barry's process of settling one's mind into a particular scene, have been crucial to my development as a fiction writer. I've found myself in other didactic settings where a prompt is more structural i.e., "write a story in a particular style where a character does something" and/or "use these words" in your story and those tend to fall flat for me. The prompt that was the genesis of "Whomp" was neither of those kinds—it came from a book, *Naming the World and other exercises for the creative writer*, edited by Bret Anthony Johnson. *Naming the World* is full of jewels if you like writing exercises. As I remember it, the prompt went something like: *What's the most terrifying story you've heard? Write it.* When I returned to the text (in the section on plot, my perennial struggle) to find the reference, I realized a few things. The author of the essay/prompt (interestingly called The Pleasure Principle) is Josh Emmons and it had three steps. I stopped after the first: "Think of the most frightening experience anyone has ever related to you and spend five to ten minutes imagining what it would have been like to be personally involved. When you have a clear idea of the narrative trajectory and have felt a frisson of the fear it inspired, write out the incident in third person, in fewer than fifteen hundred words."

I have a connection to someone whose brother died in an avalanche much in the way Logan's did. The connection was close enough that I heard the story directly, from those close to the brothers, but distant enough that I didn't know the survivor to have reached out to him directly, or to have my own sadness about it. It was a strange, vicarious trauma, one very different from those I experience regularly as a family physician when people share their stories with me. When I heard about the surviving brother's actions, they stuck with me. One of my critical curiosities as a writer relates to the choices people make and how those decisions or indecisions echo in their subsequent experience. The ski accident occurred in 2012; I can't quite say why it was the thing that popped to mind to answer Emmon's prompt in 2017, but it did and I began to write the story.

JM: Prompts can absolutely be useful for genesis, as you suggest, but I wonder about their efficacy in a classroom setting—especially one where the students are expected to read their first drafts aloud when finished. That practice seems to venerate the first draft process without much acknowledging revision and rewriting; it also prioritizes quick impulse over slow consideration—particularly when the exercise is timed. And so writers come out of those workshops with the idea that they should be able to pull great material out of thin air quickly—without thorough forethought and rewriting. These negatives have always worried me when it comes to generative exercises and workshops. But I certainly agree that there are productive prompts and less so; there's an art to every aspect of pedagogy, and it can be very difficult to pull a premise from thin air without a little help. Are prompts and secondhand stories often how you land on your premises, or do you have other methods?

LM: I agree with you about the risk of using prompts in any setting where both writing to them and sharing the results is required or expected. Generative exercises of these sorts ideally should be limited to writers who seek them out. I don't teach creative writing often, but when I do (to medical students), I tend to discourage any sharing of work. In Barry and Chaon's course, they employed a limited and strictly regimented way of sharing work. Readers were to read without editing, listeners were to listen without looking at the reader and without thinking of a reply. At the end of the reading, one of the leaders said, "Good, next," and the next person could read or pass as they wished with no remarks made. This helps, at least some, to decrease the performative aspects of group writing exercises, but I agree pitfalls remain. It is interesting to me now, to remember that "Whomp" emerged out of an exercise I gave myself and worked on alone.

And I agree completely, about how exercises can convince a writer that there's more to an early draft that might actually be there. I have heard many editors say this is one of the most common 'errors' they see with submissions from new(er) writers, and I, as a newer writer, believe that. "Whomp" required several more drafts past the one I thought was final before it found a home. And then, more revision from there.

In terms of how I've started other work, I often use news or history as a jumping off point to help me create a character. I am writing a novel that includes a storyline set in the late 1950s/early 1960s during the development of oral contraception. The idea started from a medical history museum. A one-sentence caption on one of the displays hinted (at least to me) that there might be more controversy than the curator was willing to acknowledge. It sparked my curiosity.

Many times, I'll make up a character and setting

and try to imagine them into trouble. My character generation relies heavily on what I call 'collage': taking elements of personality, age, and life circumstances from a variety of people I know or read about, then putting them together in new ways. With settings, most of my work is set in real, specific places (suburban Cleveland, Worcester, Massachusetts, Northwest Montana), though I often tweak the geography to serve my fictional purposes. I am fascinated with the intersection of the natural world's beauty and the built environment's ugliness/gaudiness/banality, and those juxtapositions recur in my fiction as well.

JM: If I may ask, what was the "surviving brother's actions" you alluded to above? How closely related is your fictional account to the secondhand story you heard?

LM: In the real-life accident, two brothers, both very experienced backcountry skiers, were out together when one was taken up by an avalanche and the other had to leave him to go for help with the knowledge that his brother would die/was dead.

In short, the fictional accident is very closely related to the real one. The remainder of the story is completely imagined, though I did work a cubicle job several years ago that helped me with that setting, and I am familiar with the more mundane aspects of death, as so many are, from the loss of my father.

JM: So there's a good bit of personal experience here mixed in with research of other experiences. I had a good laugh when you mentioned, during the revisions process, that you spent a good bit of time googling different types of cubicles. This sort of research might seem tedious, but it sure is useful for writing convincing fiction. The story appearing alongside this one, "Myopic," has an absurd amount of research put into it, so I don't want to dwell on this topic too much here, but in short, how much research goes into your fiction? You've got the call center, the avalanche, and a handful of other small events that seem to need a bit of research to convincingly portray.

LM: Early on my education as a creative writer I was introduced to the concept that in the particulars one finds the universal (google tells me this comes from Joyce and the quote is, "In the particular is contained the universal"). It was an easy concept to hold on to, as in my medical education, I had been taught that an excellent clinician is a cataloger of details, both in the patient's story, where the answers are often found from random asides, and in examination of patients, where the both gestalt and tiny details will guide you as to what's going on and how worried you need to be.

In my creation of scenes, I do a lot of sense work in my imagination.This leads me to wonder about all sorts of things, like how avalanches start and look and sound; and when you hear frogs versus bugs versus birds in the wilderness that has grown up in abandoned areas of Cleveland. As a Gen X-er who remembers the days pre-internet, I have great love and respect for the many rabbit holes I fall through on the World Wide Web (people used to really say it like that). I adore maps of all kinds but also have found online catalogs for a cubicle manufacturer, Reddit threads of heroin users offering tips for self-detox off methadone, and a blog by a musicologist who makes recordings near ponds in northeast Ohio.

So I like specifics, particularly oddball specifics. For short fiction I tend to do most of my research after I have a draft completed. For example, there really is an Aruba Lane in Fort Collins, Colorado. I think I discovered this through a combination of Zillow and Google maps. I knew Lia lived in a particular kind of housing development and I wanted her to be within a long night's drive of Logan's office. The whole subdivision is named for places in the Caribbean which I find to be absurd, hysterical, and wistful in a way that fit the tone of "Whomp" nicely. I have never been to Wyoming, but I researched bad Wyoming jokes for the saying on the mugs in the gas station.

JM: Your "particulars" is my "specificity." As you (and Joyce) suggest, there's often a misconception in young writers that vague equals universal. These writers will refuse to name their protagonists, they'll skimp on description, they'll avoid detail in the hopes that the reader will fill in the gaps with their own personal experience. These are the stories that make up the majority of what gets thrown out in the first round by our editors.

There are degrees of specificity, of course. I think of writers on the extreme end of specificity—someone like Breece D'J Pancake and the "Myopic" writer, Mason Boyles—who are wildly successful in doing so.

"Whomp" was nearly done when you submitted it—very clearly in a late draft that had been worked on significantly. Yet I noticed a couple of small plot holes and inconsistencies—I think they were all related to how the call center scenes played out—that took us out of the story. These were by and large small fixes—yet important. I made the argument that, while every story needn't be 100% realistic, it does need to abide by the laws of the world it's operating in. (Note: readers will know that none of our editors are necessarily fans of "straight realism"; one of my top ten favorite stories we've published was Megan Swenson's "Purple" in issue 7.1, which certainly was operating outside of the real world and real-world logic.) I made the case that "Whomp," however, was operating in the real world, albeit through a grieving character, so the laws we apply to this story are the laws of the real world with appropriate, grief-related allowances and grief-related breaks in realism. A plot hole about how a call center's automated messaging works isn't explained by his grief in any way, so a plot hole of this sort isn't justified by the text. You ultimately agreed and filled the small holes with some pretty sturdy cement.

All of this to say that the world a story creates determines what logic breakages the story justifies (though of course this concept, like any concept of fiction writing, could be experimented on with purpose). But I also understand your idea, which you mentioned in emails, that creation can sometimes be at odds with logic. This idea comes through more readily in poetry but is true in part for fiction, too. Could you delve into that idea a little further—continuing or correcting what I've started to get at above? For you, how is creation at odds with logic?

LM: While deliberate use of specific and peculiar detail can, I believe, make a scene come alive in a reader's imagination, there is a tension with naturalistic writing between constructing a world that a reader can inhabit and not over-explaining it. It's a landscape painting, not a set of blueprints. The distinction does not relate to the density of detail; as we have discussed, many writers use an abundance of specificity to great effect. Carrying the visual art analogy further, both Turner and Seurat painted landscapes, but the number of brushstrokes in their work differs.

I believe the 'test' for appropriate amount of detail is to determine whether they serve the narrative wholly, meaning that they work at the level of the story's logic (plausibility, sequence, rules of the world) and also the story's emotions (voice, images, language). This might not be true for everyone, but I often find that there is tension between what I am calling a story's logic and its emotion.

Finding a balance between these two poles is a critical work in revision, and as we know with "Whomp," was very much helped by multiple close readings by an editor.

JM: All precisely and concisely worded. I want to circle back to something you mentioned earlier. Your "critical curiosity" as a writer being about "the choices people make and how those decisions or indecisions echo in their subsequent experience." Have you ever seen *Force Majeure*? It's a good film with a similar setting. It also has a similar crux: the whole film focuses around a poor, split-second decision during an avalanche—and the after-effects of that poor decision. The director of the film, Ruben Ostlund, also directed a favorite of mine, *The Square*. Though of course *Force Majeure* has a very different decision that plays out in very different ways from "Whomp," you may want to check it out considering your thematic focus.

It isn't often a writer states their exact thematic preoccupations. With your thematic concerns here clearly in the forefront of your brain, do you intentionally approach stories with this thematic goal in mind? Does being hyperaware of your thematic preoccupations only strengthen the authority and themes of your work, or does it have downsides as well?

LM: I do not approach stories with a thematic or narrative goal in mind. Rather, I start with a question or premise. Sometimes I start with only a voice and setting and the conflicts emerge organically. A premise can serve as a prompt, a jumping off point, and soon after, I let the early part of the story dictate the story's logic or contract. With "Whomp" I was initially curious about Logan's decision on the mountain (to go for help, in the vein of self-preservation, instead of risking an attempt at rescue), but as the story evolved, it was less about that decision itself, and about how having made it impacts a person. The more I thought about it, the more I believe what Logan says to himself at the end: that decisions like these are being made all the time, and his was the rare one that showed.

That "critical curiosity" statement is a summary judgement based on reading and re-reading my work and trying to understand what question the story is trying to address (which often isn't the question I started with). Perhaps it comes from having written too many artist statements on residency and fellowship applications. On the other hand, I think being able to step back and read one's work with distance is extraordinarily helpful in revision. Once I knew "Whomp" was a story about grief (rather than guilt, shame, or fatalism) I was able to revise the manuscript so that the subtext underscored the theme. But revising for theme, for me, has to come very late in the process or else it won't work. The changes that emerge from a revision pass for theme are subtle—word substitutions, manipulations of pacing, focused compression or expansion. If you try to force theme (and, for that matter, subtext) on a manuscript too early, to my mind, it simply won't work.

JM: All that makes sense to me, though certainly other writers will have other approaches. Let's talk a little more about the structure, which you noted above you found a little later in drafting. Your story bounces back and forth in time—between the day of the avalanche and the weeks following it—whereas a more conventional story might've just stuck with one or the other, then progressed linearly. Why did you decide on sliding the earlier moments in? I think it succeeds in building the tension throughout the piece.

LM: Thanks. When I first began drafting, I had scenes with Logan at work, thinking about the avalanche. The draft demonstrated a classic new writer narrative problem a teacher of mine calls a "sipping coffee and staring out the window story." I needed to give the protagonist some present action, which is where his first call with Lia came in. I love stories where we see people doing the activities of their so-called ordinary lives and activities of the mind (memory, longing, self-deceit, fantasy) start to play over or under the main action like a second tune. Grief is such an intrusive experience, and unpredictable, which made it seem plausible that Logan's story of the avalanche returns to him over time. In an early draft, the narrator directly addressed the constructed nature of his story about the avalanche, saying things like "in my story" and "when I told it" when he spoke of the day of his brother's death. These moments of direct address were cut as I revised (they threw the reader out of the fictive dream and how others perceived his telling and the experience became less important to the present day timeline), but a few remained. Once I had a thread of narrative action in the present time, it was a matter of finding places where his grief and memories overpowered him and made him essentially flashback to the avalanche. Another teacher, Nancy Zafris, taught the deft use of backstory with the maxim, "plant, deepen, return" where you give backstory in a way that it has its own narrative tension. One important aspect of structure that was in place early was the placement of the Aidan's death at the beginning. The story is not about the mystery of what happened to Aidan, but how Logan's experience and actions have begun to change who he is.

JM: That "coffee cup remembrance" story structure you describe is typical in submissions: a passive, interiority-swamped frontstory that looks back on a more active backstory—a writer choosing the wrong period of time to focus their story on, and a passive frontstory that only serves to ruminate on past events. I'm glad you found a way to build out the frontstory in a convincing way and avoid this pitfall so successfully; in "Whomp," the frontstory is just as active as the backstory, if not moreso.

During revision, you mentioned the useful phrase "thematic currency." We were talking about the paragraph where Logan begins with, "here's what I think," then speaks a little bit to the themes of the story, specifically regards decision making. This is an important thematic paragraph, and you worked hard to cut thematic language throughout the story in order to save your "thematic currency" for this paragraph of interiority. Could you speak to this moment and the idea of "thematic currency"?

LM: Yes, we were discussing the utility (or lack) of places where Logan breaks the fourth wall, ever so slightly, to talk to a reader. Initially, I thought of these moments as no different than internal monologue, but as written they had heightened syntax and a more philosophical tone than the rest. As I mentioned above, early in the drafting the "I" narrator was very self-conscious of the notion that all conversation, even internal conversation and memory, is constructed as narrative. It called too much attention to itself. The draft that made it to you at *Driftwood* had been scoured of most these intrusions, but three remained. We decided to cut all but the final one.

The moment where Logan says to himself "here's what I think" comes late in the story and might serve as an anti-epiphany. My thinking was, if the reader has come with me this far, I can put this *big idea* out there and they might, (1) read it as something Logan is really saying to himself on the side of the road in a nondescript housing development and possibly considering saying to Lia in his speech; and/or (2) allow a brief digression into writerliness as the story reaches its climax. In coming to this decision, we discussed the concept of authorial capital, meaning (I am making this up) the amount of obvious writerly stuff a reader will let you get away with in a given narrative. This would vary a lot from piece to piece, but in a realist story with a narrator whose voice and insights are flattened by grief and guilt, I chose to spend my limited currency on that paragraph where I felt like the expansive language was working on multiple levels. The moments that were cut, didn't 'weigh' that much in the story, and therefore weren't worth the expense.

JM: Many stories have this sort of paragraph you describe: fiction's equivalent of a thesis statement, usually moored in interiority. We could debate all day the pros and cons of this paragraph, and most writers will stand pretty firmly on one side or the other of whether a story *ever* has enough "thematic currency" to get away with a paragraph like this, but the frank truth is that—like it or hate it—many, many stories rely on this thematic unifying/concluding paragraph, which often appears around three-fourths into a story. Could you explain, for our readers, the idea of an "anti-epiphany" and how it worked in "Whomp"?

LM: I have limited education in literature, so please forgive the lack of detail or precision here, but let's say Joycean epiphany is a moment (usually near the end of the story or scene) where a character gains a deeper insight into the reality or meaning of things or events (often with religious or spiritual overtones). In "Whomp," the moment where Logan can no longer turn back from his odd journey in search of Lia serves as an instance where the character realizes there is no deeper insight to be gained. No matter how much he or others try to project meaning onto the decision he made on the mountain, it was simply one decision of the millions that we make over a lifetime. Though it might have had huge implications (the ending of his own life, for example), he can never know this for sure, just as none of us can know the real consequences our actions or non-actions have. So, it's *anti-* in the sense that the moment is one where the character realizes there is no guiding or overarching order to life's vicissitudes. Somewhere in my recent doomscrolling, the universe served me (irony intended) a link to a 2015 essay reprinted in LitHub about Frost's "The Road Not Taken" (the essay is called "You're Probably Misreading Robert Frost's Most Famous Poem"). It's a much more nuanced discussion of some of the same ol' existential crisis business that I was swimming in with this story.

JM: Let's get into the minutia for a moment before I hit you with our usual final few questions in a sort of lighting round. At *Driftwood Press*, we're not usually fans of comma splices, but I think you made a good case for using them well with this example. "My mind is playing tricks, but it doesn't matter, it puts me back on the mountain." The emotion in this line catches us by surprise. You mentioned to me privately that you preferred comma splices to semicolons. Could you speak a little to punctuation decisions in "Whomp"? Do they shift from story to story, scene to scene, or are your punctuation decisions relatively consistent throughout your different works of fiction?

LM: My initial reaction is to just put my hands up, yell "Busted," and confess that, for a creative writer, I have a very tenuous connection to grammar. It's true that my fundamental education in writing was in social science, and to a lesser degree, natural science, and though it may sound judgmental, it has been my experience that readers of grant proposals, research reports, and policy papers accept a wider range of punctuation as correct than do readers of literature. So I come to creative writing with somewhat hampered fundamentals, which partially explains my love of the comma splice. This is not an altogether helpful insight.

When I began to study creative writing in earnest (in my late thirties), I wrote poetry, essays, and fiction in equal measure. The ear training I had in poetry workshops forms the basis for how I make punctuation decisions. Most of my fiction starts out strongly connected to voice, even if it doesn't always stay that way. I tend to use punctuation as rest notations in music—they suggest to a reader how to pace out the words. The next step is to look at what I have and revise into functional, logical sentences. This might be unnecessary for many, but it is a key step for me. From there, I read aloud over and over, and experiment with different versions. I love an em dash, likely because I fear the semicolon, which reminds me of technical and professional writing. For longer short stories, I tend to use punctuation, sentence length, and paragraphing in a way similar to "Whomp." When I am writing flash fiction or nonfiction, I tend to be more experimental in general, including with punctuation choices.

JM: I'm not sure you give yourself enough credit here, Lynda. Your thorough consideration above signals you as a careful writer. But I do hope you overcome your semicolon fear; they're brilliantly useful, and their long history of usage in modern literature—from *Moby-Dick* to Faulkner—signals them as not belonging to technical writing, though I've heard that concern before from submitters.

LM: Thanks, and yes, I don't mean to virtue signal humility, but I haven't before been asked many of these questions. It's been challenging and fulfilling to explain my own process, and therefore come to understand it more thoroughly.

JM: Let's jump into a little lightning round—a handful of questions that I try to ask most of our writers. First up, is there anything unique about your personal writing process?

LM: It's not unique, but I am on team handwriting. All my initial drafts are written in quick, barely legible (even to me) scrawl in spiral notebooks that I buy on sale at back-to-school time. I then type, which gives me an early second pass on the text. I credit my zealousness about drafting longhand to Lynda Barry and Dan Chaon, but I was already inclined that way before I took their course.

JM: What was the hardest part of writing "Whomp"?

LM: Getting the tone of the present-day narrative right. I wanted it to be weird, but not too weird. My favorite stories are ones that are naturalistic but strange, where you can inhabit the consciousness of a character whose perceptions and interpretations of the events are just to the left of what's expected or normal.

JM: Do you think of yourself as belonging to any particular tradition? If so, who are your masters and who are your contemporaries?

LM: I have struggled mightily to answer this question, which led me to an internal inquiry as to why I found it so challenging. I think it's because I don't yet have a handle on what tradition I might belong to. Others, when they hear that I write fiction and know my other profession, will sometimes ask, "like Atul Gawande or Michael Crichton?," and if I am bold, I'll answer "more like Chekhov." But I have only read Chekhov in translation and would never compare myself. Even though much of my writing concerns medicine, healthcare, and illness, I think being a doctor-writer is the least interesting part of my identity.

I tend to read and love writers that I cannot compare myself to, like Jesmyn Ward and Mohsin Hamid. I simply need to read more to have a firm answer, but I might orbit around writers like Grace Paley, Charles Baxter, and Jane Smiley. Dean Bakopoulos's novels *Don't Come Back from the Moon* and *Summerlong* combine humor, tenderness, and longing in a way I admire. He has been a teacher, and I sought him out because of how evocative I find his writing.

In terms of contemporaries, I was struck by Chris Cander's recent debut novel, *The Weight of a Piano* and RL Maizes's story collection, *We Love Anderson Cooper*. I have the great fortune to be in a writing group with, among others, Mary Grimm, whose June 2019 *New Yorker* story, "Back Then," is fantastic (listen to The Writer's Voice podcast for her Ohio accent) and Laura Maylene Walter, whose debut novel *Body of Stars* is forthcoming in Spring 2021. The group has helped me so much, but none of us writes similarly to the others.

JM: What other mediums have influenced your work? How?

LM: For aspects of structure and craft I lean heavily on other arts, particularly painting and music. In another life, I'd have been an art history major. I am lucky to live near a premier art museum and I like to lose myself in the works there. I think a lot about the process of painting (though I know little) as I construct fiction. Other times, the metaphor of music composition helps me to make decisions about my stories. I also lean heavily on my identity as a physician. I mine that life for content, of course, but being trained as a clinician involves developing one's powers of observation and discernment particularly as it relates to people's bodies, words, and actions. I know that the sensory skills I use in medicine help me to imagine the rich and specific details that we discussed as being crucial for inviting a reader into one's narrative.

JM: Where can readers find more of your work? Have you been published before?

LM: "Whomp" is my second full-length short story published, though I've also published a work of pandemic-related flash fiction, as well as essays, interviews, and an excerpt (audio) from my unpublished first novel. I have a website where much of the work is linked (lyndamontgomery.org).

JM: What are you working on now?

LM: More short stories about odd people suffering and surviving ordinary lives. My current short fiction project was inspired in part by the medical office building where I work two days a week. It's like a time capsule from 1989, with mirrored glass windows and wall panels and a four-story atrium filled with formica and silk plants including a 25-foot tall artificial palm tree. Note we are in Northeast Ohio. I am also at work on a second novel, a more straightforward realist story of two women physicians, one is a med student in 2017-2019, the other is an OB/Gyn who directed some of the first long-term clinical trials of oral contraceptive pills in late 1950s/early 1960s Puerto Rico.

JM: And how's it going?

LM: Well, that's always an interesting question. I am excited about the novel and got nearly to the end of a first draft before putting it aside this past summer. Then, let's blame 2020, I found it difficult to keep my mind in it as a novel requires. The current story is a discontinuous narrative that I have worked on in between other things, but I think I am close to having the full story down. One thing I'll say: the longer I write, the more patient I am with how long it takes to get to a finished product. It's a huge thrill to publish fiction, but being content with the process is necessary for being content with living an artistic life.

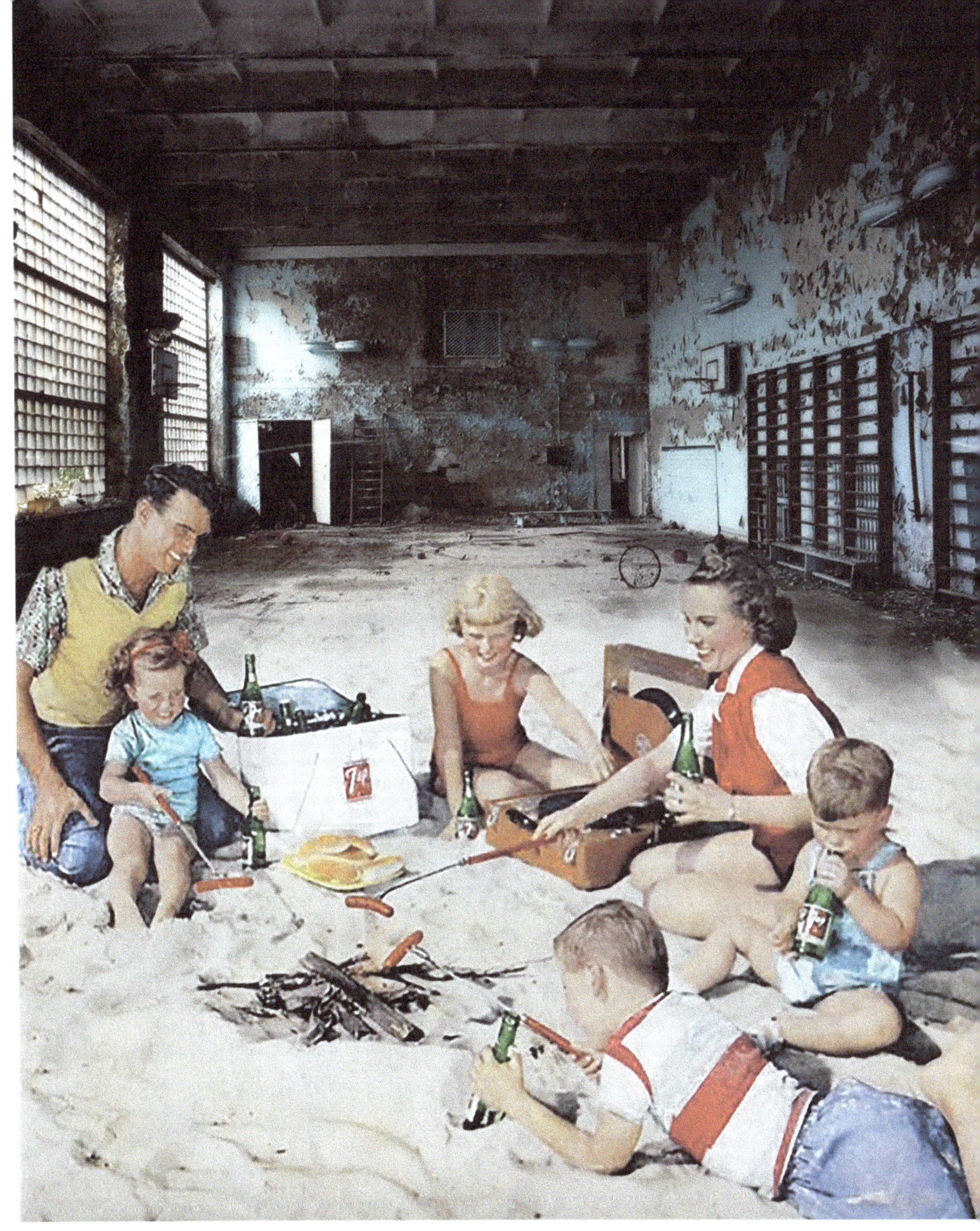

SAM HEYDT'S
FAMILY PICNIC

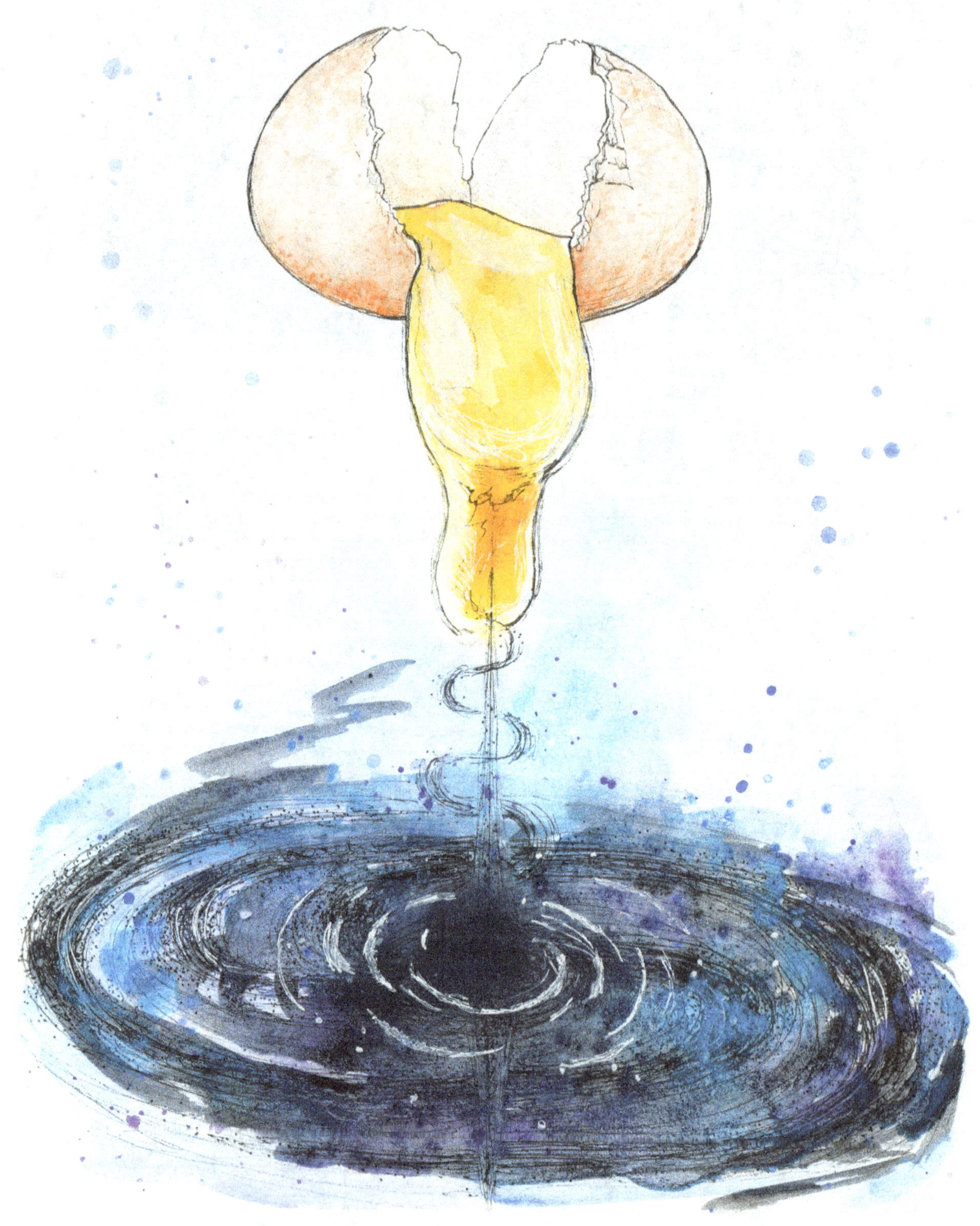

My Mother Checks a Carton of Eggs to See if Any are Broken

ROBIN GOW

Pressing my finger
into the skulls of eggs.

Heads of babies are soft
and not like eggs. They wouldn't crack—
they have no shells.

There is my mother with
two and a half songs—
two and half songs, I mean.

I bite down on planets and
they smash like eggs and I apologize
to the mother

in the dead supermarket
who will find all her planets
synonyms for "smashed"

see: shatter, splinter.

Who will find her one son
split in half with a daughter.

He is hiding inside an egg carton.

Yolk all cosmic
with memories. How dare
I swallow all that for myself.

But the problem is I'm hungry
and there's nothing
I can do about that.

My stomach
is a baby or maybe there's
a baby in my stomach,
Men get pregnant all
the time you just don't care about them.

Black holes can't get pregnant but

they can hold all kinds
of pieces of bodies.

I juggle heart beats
like eggs. They all splinter

on a sidewalk.

I juggle planets and catch
them in my mouth—
eating them
shells and all.

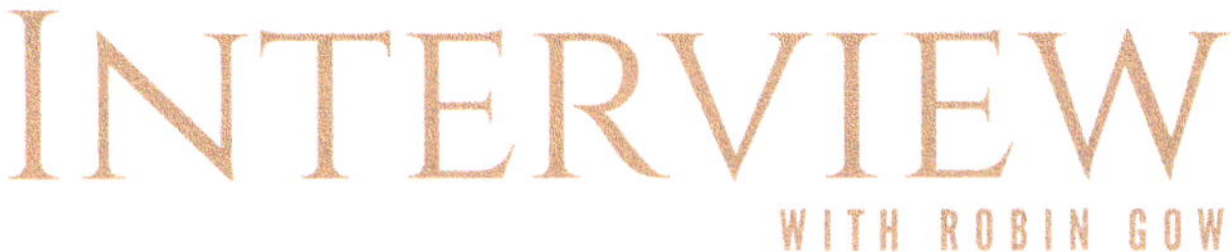

What inspired the poem?

I went to the grocery store with my mom and I watched her open the carton to check if any eggs were broken. She lifted each egg so gently and carefully. When I write, I usually try to follow the associations that come and go from there. I thought about eggs, then ovaries, and then this idea of fertility. I think the word "inspired" is really vague and so is "empowered," but I feel inspired and empowered by pregnant men and I guess that's kind of where the poem landed.

What was the hardest part about writing it?

This poem comes from a collection that I never intended to be about being trans. I was writing, trying to conjure the voice of a black hole and trans stuff kept coming further and further forward in the poems. I felt frustrated. I'm really happy being a trans person, so sometimes I worry about writing trauma, but I couldn't really control where the poems took me. This poem is part of that because I love my mom a lot and it's hard to reflect on myself early in coming out as trans when no one really saw me—especially not my family.

How much revision went into this poem?

A whole lot. I'm not a big reviser (not because I think they don't need it) but because I have these feelings of inadequacy when I revise. I really have to thank Judy Baumel, my former professor/friend, for her thoughts that helped me get through revising a lot of poems like this that feel very vulnerable.

Is there anything unique about your personal writing process?

I have written a poem a day since New Year's 2017 and have not skipped a day. It's less of a dedication and more of an obsession. Or, I guess in another frame, it's kind of a way of grounding myself.

How long do you usually spend working on a single poem?

This is hard to say. Sometimes when I revise, I don't think it's the same poem, so I guess I'd say probably fifteen minutes for a version of a poem. I can't take longer or else I can't hold onto the idea long enough to finish the poem. I drink a lot of coffee in the morning and sprint whatever ideas I have each day.

Who are some of your favorite poets?

This is so hard. Just to list three I read recently and am obsessed with: Justin Phillip Reed, Monica McClure, and Zaina Alsous.

How would you personally define poetry?

A feeling and then sharing it. My friend Rachel Stempel and my partner Benny Sisson often will say "that's a poem" about day-to-day stuff as a joke, but I genuinely think those are poems even if they are brief and only known to us and not written down.

Where can readers find more of your work?

On my website (frobingowpoetry.wordpress.com) or twitter (@Gow_Robin_Frank).

Things That Remind You of Your Friends' Dead Dads

Lina Patton

Doing crunches. Not the regular kind, but the twisted ones: left elbow to right knee, right elbow to left knee, back and forth, like you're throwing a tantrum. He coached your JV soccer team. He had a beautiful face and blond hair. He'd smile and say come on, girls, just a few more.

The number 23. So much so that anytime you see it, you have to whisper, 24, just to feel like you're moving past. It was his race car number. He crashed when you were in the third grade. You bought his daughter a stuffed elephant because at nine years old, what else would you do?

Valentine's Day. This is a new one. Your upstairs neighbor, your new friend, said she hated the holiday, the day her dad finally died. She wears his Soviet belt buckle sometimes. Now, on February 14th, you think of him, of the Russians, as you smell your flowers.

Getting popcorn kernels stuck in your teeth. One afternoon in kindergarten, you were at your friend's house and her dad was drunk (you won't realize till later). He was convinced she had a piece of popcorn stuck in her bottom incisor. He made her sit down, open wide, as he leaned over her mouth with a toothpick. It was funny at the time. You all laughed.

Hockey games. Any of them. He was your neighbor and coached the U Maine team. You and your friend loved the arena—the icy stale air, the loud chants and painted faces. You ran around the rink drinking giant sodas and eating bright orange nachos. When he died, you and she walked her dog around the block. She cried and you felt bad you didn't.

Subway. The sandwiches. He'd pick her up from basketball practice carrying those thin, swinging plastic bags. Later, when he shoots himself in the mouth off the running trail, that's what you think of first. You were in high school then. This one hurt the most.

You imagine they barely knew your name. You imagine you barely knew theirs. This was how it was supposed to be—meaning nothing to each other.

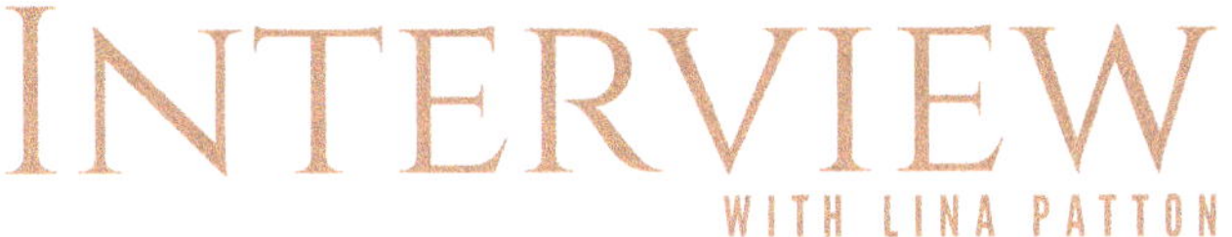

INTERVIEW
WITH LINA PATTON

What inspired the poem?

I've always been interested in the instinctive nature of memory, the way some details stick with us—reminding us of some person or place or time—in ways we cannot control. It's so interesting to me that while we can try to commit certain things to memory, there is no way to "forget" something, and often times, what ends up staying with us for life operates on a more subconscious, random level.

On the flip side, it's also interesting to think about what reminds other people of us, even those we barely know. I like to think there are details that bring each of us back to one another in unlikely ways, linking us all in a strange network of memory. I know this isn't a new idea, but it still feels timelessly romantic—and always brings me back to Frank O'Hara's "Personal Poem" and the line, "I wonder if one person out of the 8,000,000 is / thinking of me."

What came easiest when writing this poem?

In a way, it was cathartic to write this poem. So many moments remind me of so many various people, but these specific memories always moved me in a different way. I think it has to do with the degree of separation I had with these fathers—the way they barely skimmed my life—as well as the weight of being reminded of their untimely deaths. It felt freeing to write down these strange and sad memories that come back to me so regularly, and I hope, in a small way, it also honors the memory of them.

Who are some of your favorite poets?

Dorianne Laux, Sharon Olds, Ada Limón, Jenny Xie, and Valencia Robins.

Do you work in any other artistic mediums? If so, how do those other genres inform your poetry?

I write mainly fiction, but I have the greatest respect for poetry. I'm in awe of the way a few well-placed words and lines can pack so much emotion, and I admire poetry's lyricism and music. Even now as I work on a novel, I start each writing day by reading a handful of poems because it helps put me in the right emotional space and reminds me to pay attention to my sentences. As a result, I'd have to say poetry informs my fiction more than the other way around. But most of my poems do come from moments, images, or details that I do not feel are right for a story, so there is that connection. For me, both come down to the same practice of observation, and I'm grateful to work in both genres.

How would you personally define poetry?

One of my favorite professors, the late Alan Cheuse, used to say, "you are never more alive than in the moment after you finish a poem." So I think, then, I would define poetry as an illumination of life? Although that sounds far cheesier. Let's stick with Alan's words.

What is the best piece of writing advice you've been given?

Keep going. Embrace failure. The ones who will make it are the ones who will not give up.

It's easy to hear that advice and shrug it off, because I know we hear it all the time, but as a writer, you really have to feel it; you really have to accept it. What they don't tell you outright, and what takes time to admit, is that you are not the exception. Maybe you need to believe that for a little while, maybe you need that motivation, but get over it quickly. I promise it's better on the other side.

[IN NEPAL, YOU LEARN IT TAKES]

LORA KINKADE

in nepal, you learn it takes

one thousand pounds of wood

to burn a body.

in california,

i consider swimming.

polish a coffee with my shirtsleeve.

growl at the dog until she pants.

with every step, someone came before you

to build that step. yr father

’s shitting himself but yr

loving it.

cold clear lake. the peasants gathering

to view their own mountain.

you always called it your mountain.

you always hated my interrupting

chats with your mum.

/

1048

, one thousand

pounds of unambiguous flesh.

my bright, unconquerable shoulders.

the public lunge & tackle, the rabble, a parrot

to each strange & veined arm.

/

you let the cat

eat the bromeliad

& thought nothing of it. you lied

once a day

like a multivitamin

& thought

nothing

of it.

you were my cake & i ate him too.

sucked him off while you

changed our sheets. thought about your mountain.

watched the pointed shadows a skull can make.

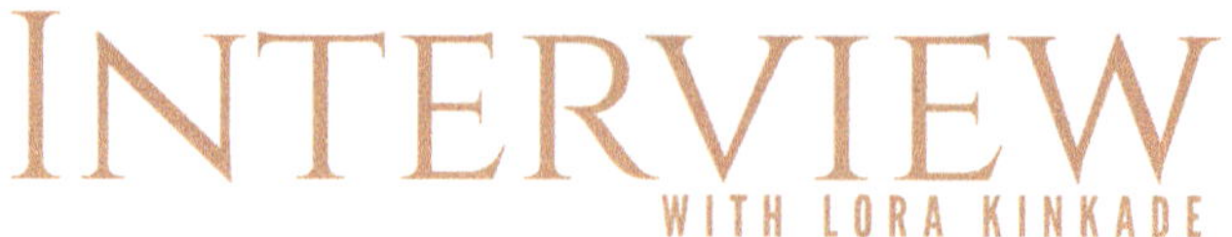

What inspired the poem?

Mainly a reckoning with a former partner's narcissism. The vignettes that make up cohabitation. The substantive moments that led to and chronicled our falling out, apart.

What was the hardest part about writing it?

Deciding how to separate the distinct vignette-formally. Also the sexual language. It can be challenging and vulnerable to allow something so explicit to remain on the page and in the final edit. I think, too, it can be challenging to deal with an event or image that is recurring within the scope of your work. This poem contains one such moment. I have to ask myself whether I'm using the moment to take up space or to move me from one moment to the next (because I am familiar and comfortable with how to handle it) or if it is appearing in a distinct, alive, and productive way.

What came easiest when writing this poem?

The first section or vignette came fairly easily. Some first lines appear entire and whole in your mind's eye, and the first line of this poem was one such line. What came after came fairly easily until the poem transitioned and then lost some momentum.

Was there anything in your original conception that did not make it in?

Likely, although I didn't retain any former drafts, which I only do when the changes are not substantial. Some poems feel like easy births and this poem was that.

How much revision went into this poem?

Most of the revision was formal. I think I played most with line breaks, because I wanted to be conscious of the specific speed of each section and how moments and language were being fractured and fragmented by the enjambment. Several of the line breaks are fairly disruptive and will likely rub some readers the wrong way. So I spent a substantial amount of time with these moments.

Is this poem categorical of your work? Why or why not?

In some ways, yes. I've been working with this form for some time now—double spaced lines—and there are other choices, the spelling of "yr" for example, which are recurring within my work. Much of my work deals with the juxtaposition of the violence of the natural world and/or the agricultural world with the quieter but equally impactful violences of interpersonal, familial, and inner conflict.

What is your favorite line from the poem or the line you are most proud of?

I think my favorite line is "with every step, someone came before you / to build that step." It felt like the greatest moment of growth, understanding, or potential for me while I was writing it. It was the moment I unconsciously look for when I'm writing wherein something transfigures or reframes.

How long do you usually spend working on a single poem?

It really depends. Sometimes a poem comes out easily and other times it's more of a labor. Anywhere from one hour to two or three to write—and then revision can take another several. I think I revise a lot less than other poets, perhaps to my detriment. I feel concerned about taking away from the sort of "essence" a poem contains in its nascency by revisiting it with different attention/intentions.

How long have you been writing poetry? What has changed from your first poem to your newest work?

I've been writing poetry since I was five or six, but I didn't start writing it consistently until we watched *Shakespeare in Love* in the 9th grade and I thought it was so sexy I just had to learn how to write in iambic pentameter. I wrote exclusively sonnets in iambic pentameter for years and then transitioned to free verse in college, when I discovered there were living poets.

Who are some of your favorite poets?

Jorie Graham, Joanna Klink, Jericho Brown, Ocean Vuong, Ilya Kaminsky, Diana Khoi Nguyen, Buddy Wakefield, Jos Charles, Adrienne Rich, and Sharon Olds.

If you had to narrow it down, what three books have had the most impact on your writing?

Diving into the Wreck, by Adrienne Rich. *Ariel*, by Sylvia Plath. E.E. Cummings' *Selected Poems*.

How would you personally define poetry?

A mechanism that reinvigorates and reincarnates language and therefore wakes us back up to the experience of being human.

Based on your personal experience, what advice would you give to other writers?

Find someone(s) to share your work with. Witness is a hugely important part of creation, and the accountability and recognition of a peer group can sustain momentum in the daily practice.

What is the best piece of writing advice you've been given?

Surprise yourself. If you aren't being surprised in the process of writing, you're not engaging the poem (or yourself) fully.

Where can readers find more of your work?

Several of my poems can be found in *Damaged Goods Press'* recent anthology *The Impossible Beast,* the 40th edition of *The Bombay Gin* and *Ursus Americanus Press' Landfill Journal.*

What drew you to *Driftwood Press*?

The stunning visual art and scope of each issue. Their interest in investigating the poetic process and lending some transparency to the inception of a body of work.

No Man's Land

SUMMER J. HART

She picks a sequin off the mauve & cream striped cushion, threads a white dog's hair through the hole in the center, folds it in half, & flicks it against the trailer wall.

He is telling her about the family business, one arm slung across the back of the sofa as casual as denim, the other nervous at his knee. She crosses her arms, tucks her hands into the opposite sleeves of her t-shirt.

Sparkle can light a cigarette with her vagina, he says, handing her his sweater.

///

They spend the day wandering in the woods behind the motel, crystallized dirt splintering under their sneakers. *This*, he says, *is unorganized territory—a no man's land—beyond jurisdiction.*

She imagines him striking a match.

Leaves whip at their ankles. A pale dog follows, slipping in & out of the white space between trees. Its movements are lawless, precise.

///

Taillights in the parking lot signal dawn. She unrolls her sleeping bag.

You know I'll always love you, he whispers, *no matter what.*

She draws her tongue across the front of her teeth.

Smoke curls in under the doorframe.

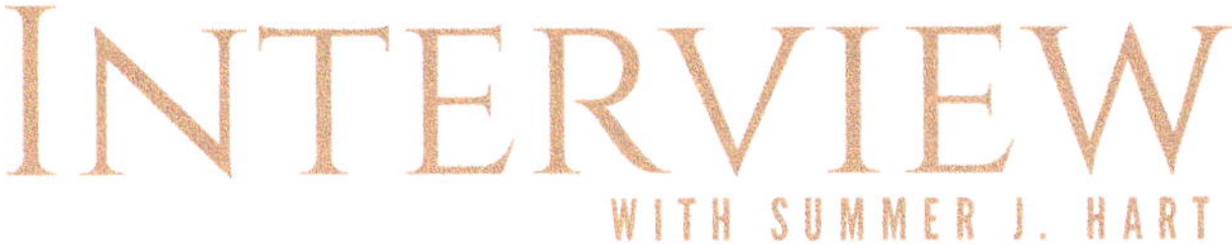

INTERVIEW
WITH SUMMER J. HART

What inspired the poem?

This poem was inspired in part by learning about unorganized territories in between towns in northern Maine and a boy who lived in one.

How long do you usually spend working on a single poem?

It depends on the poem. Sometimes, a single train ride will do it. Usually, though, it takes several weeks, countless drafts, days agonizing over one word, a stretch of time where it is completely forgotten about, a stretch of time where it is completely written off, and then one really good writing day.

How long have you been writing poetry? What has changed from your first poem to your newest work?

Although there has always been a narrative component to my work, I have only been writing poetry seriously for the last couple of years. I started by tapping thoughts in the notes app on my phone. During my commute from my village in the Hudson Valley to my job in the city, I'd start with a list, or an observation. I counted the birds I saw over the river: two herons, one eagle, seven gulls, that sort of thing. Then it would maybe turn into a haiku. I found the wild, deciduous riverscapes, and rolling banks of the Hudson inspiring.

The first poems I published were drafted in response to a call put out in 2019 by *Northern New England Review*. The theme was "True North," and it got me writing a series of prose poems based loosely on my childhood in Maine.

I shift around a bit with form, but overall my work is still very much occupied with place, superstition, and family lore.

Who are some of your favorite poets?

Octavio Paz, Louise Erdrich, Anne Carson, Sandra Simons, and Louise Glück.

Do you work in any other artistic mediums? If so, how do those other genres inform your poetry?

Yes! I am an interdisciplinary artist. I trained in book arts and printmaking but work in many mediums. I have most recently been creating immersive installations out of hand-cut paper, light, and sound.

I think of my written and visual work as coming from the same hometown, but they are not companions to each other. My installations are nature based—alluding to elements of the forest and the sea. Likewise, my poems are often set in the rivers and pines of northern Maine. Many of my visual art works share titles or lines from poems, but I have yet to combine the practices directly. You can view my artwork on my website (summerjhart.com).

What is the best piece of writing advice you've been given?

The best advice was actually more of an acknowledgement. I was having dinner with some established and very new (to me) poet friends. They shared stories about their experiences: their rejections and successes, anecdotes about presses losing (then finding!) their poems in email threads or down the backs of sofas. It helped to humanize the whole process for me.

PROMISE

R.C. DAVIS

I promise never to charge
my phone on the rim of the bathtub
or cut off my finger tips
with a kitchen knife. If I know
one thing, it's how to touch

the wax of a mosquito candle without
feeling any burn. This summer,
the dog eats cicadas in the grass
and I dream that I'm a duck
or something else with wings

(In the end I am swallowed once again
by my own skin, riding a bicycle backwards
down a hill). In a poem that isn't
this one, I keep asking
for my parents' pride

to never change its shape. I ask
the birds and each blade
of grass, mostly my own mouth
in the mirror. Canyon of teeth
singing a song too low

for my vocal range. Someday,
I will tattoo a window
on each of my shoulders. To let some light in,
I suppose, like a pair of glasses
in a movie, setting fire to a leaf.

Dollop of sun then everything
begins burning. I'm not sure
what I'm supposed to taste when
we say words like *future*. I promise you,
that if I ever have a child of my own

my hands won't shake so much
that I drop them on the tile. I'll remember
some of the words of my father's
lullabies. We'll count
the dead flies on the windowsill,

then I'll turn over a tree stump
and show the swarm
underneath. *Look, the moon is a paper plate*
that's been lit on fire. Watch it
curl into a toenail clipping.

Watch the night swallow
us in our pajama pants
and whispers. Today,
what I'm asking
is for my parents to call me *son*

before one of us is dead.
If you look directly at the sun
it leaves blue spots everywhere
and I'm sitting here, painting my nails
with the blood from my mosquito bites.

INTERVIEW

WITH R.C. DAVIS

What inspired the poem?

I first came to the poem, "Promise" with the idea of my parents and promises. What do I need to promise them and what can't I promise them? This poem begins with a series of promises to my parents before engaging with the question of how their perception of me will change as I grow older and become a truer version of myself. Turning to the subject of an imaginary future child was not something I expected when I sat down to write this poem, but it definitely makes sense within this poem's engagement with my fears and uncertainties.

What was the hardest part about writing it?

The hardest parts about writing "Promise" were finding a connection between the beginning of the poem and the section where I imagine my future child, and finding a way to land the poem at its ending. The line, "I'm not sure / what I'm supposed to taste when / we say words like *future*," was initially in the penultimate stanza, but I moved it earlier in the poem to serve as a transition to looking forward. The ending of "Promise" was something I spent a lot of time considering. This poem wandered a lot on the page and touched a lot of images and ideas, and I knew I couldn't end it with an easy conclusion. In an earlier draft, I ended with "Today, what I'm asking is for my parents to call me *son* before one of us is dead," but that line as an ending felt too conclusive to me and didn't reflect the landscape of the rest of the poem. I chose to end on the lines I did, "...and I'm sitting here, painting my nails / with the blood with my mosquito bites," because I wanted to leave the reader with an emotionally complex image and a note of questioning.

Is this poem categorical of your work? Why or why not?

I think that "Promise" represents the more surreal of my work and wanders between ideas more than most of my poetry. My relationship with my family and my wonderings about the future are themes that keep showing up in my writing again and again, and this is not the first or last poem I've written addressing my future child. Images that I'm obsessed with in my poetry, including insects and teeth, show up in "Promise" as well.

What is your favorite line from the poem or the line you are the most proud of?

"Someday, / I will tattoo a window / on each of my shoulders," is probably the line in "Promise" that I'm most proud of. It paints a memorable image and I like the way it interjects this poem's thinking and leads into the next stanza. This "someday" marks the beginning of this poem's turn towards the future, and I think this line captures this poem's surreal wondering.

How long have you been writing poetry? What has changed from your first poem to your newest work?

I've been writing poetry since my freshman year of high school, and though themes of identity and use of insect imagery are present in my poetry both then and now, my voice as a writer has certainly developed. Now, two years later, I'm more comfortable with non-linear narratives in my writing and jumping between images, and am less concerned with making a clear, overarching point in each poem. I've learned to embrace the conversational quirks in my writing style, and to embrace complexity and self-questioning in every poem I write.

Who are some of your favorite poets?

Some of my favorite poets are Sam Sax, Hieu Minh Nguyen, Ari Banias, and Jericho Brown.

MURDER

BEN KLINE

I nailed the panes / salted the hardwood beneath / around the bed / per the flyleaf notes / folded in great grand Nana's vellum bible / If I did not / the murder would / jimmy the locks / sail my breath / What are you / Who is he / I folded my lips in / Why do you / I spoke no names / That rusty afternoon / they found me / back against a red maple / grunting into my hand / calling for God / I could not see / what they slipped in my ribs / Frayed primary / silken covert / toothy blade / another bad idea / Who is he / they had heard before

After months / of winter nights / my jaw ached at waking / I stowed my lost teeth / in clean socks / I pulverized them / for the floor / I wrote no notes / burned my clipped nails / collected curls from the sink / pillows / underwear / If I did not / they would / Coal beaks / gnawing cuticle / oil / DNA / loose in the wind / above the west field / blue timothy swaying / too close to the creek / It swelled every May / overt / but forgetful

When they came / two at each window / heads twisting to see / I covered my face / I bit my tongue / What are you / more rust / Who is he / I pulled the hammer / from under / two sheets / my quilt / Why do I / its weight on my chest / lingering / like him / No name / Why am I / waiting for them / to caw / to scratch / Most violence / I have heard before / flutters / unnamed

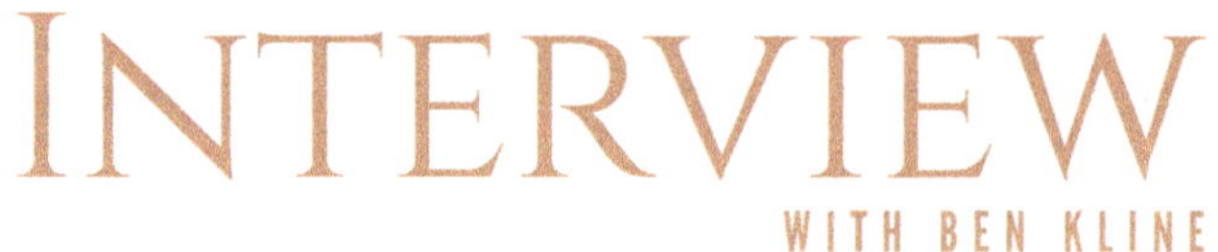

Interview

WITH BEN KLINE

What inspired the poem?

Crows. I've had a lifelong fascination with them. Back home on the farm, folks treated them with equal parts respect, fear, annoyance, and disgust. I preferred respect and fear, the folklore and superstition surrounding them. Their knowing eyes and social behavior with humans and other birds. The original draft of this poem, eight years in the making, was called "Corvus."

What was the hardest part about writing it?

Finding its marrow. For several years, the original poem was a long, sprawling thing filled with lines spent on superstition and spells and magic. The version published here is the fifty-sixth. It took time and helpful beta readers to find the core and both expose it and understand it.

What came easiest when writing this poem?

The imagery. Especially the magic stuff about salting the floor and pulverizing teeth.

Was there anything in your original conception that did not make it in?

That could be an entire essay. Mostly extraneous narrative about the crow bringing gifts and interacting with ravens and an entire middle section about hair and puberty.

Is this poem categorical of your work? Why or why not?

Thematically, yes. It features some of my favorite things to poem: folklore, identity, secrets, religion, faith, men and how rotten they are. Stylistically, no. I write a lot of prose poems, but not like this. I wrote a few poems employing these slashes and the interrupted rhythm a couple of summers ago. Almost all of them have been published now. Maybe I should write more of them.

What is your favorite line from the poem or the line you are most proud of?

Oh, the last one: "Most violence / I have heard before / flutters / unnamed." Which was the last thing written for the poem in this final version, replacing the original last line (original as in an eight-year-old first draft) that now concludes the second stanza.

Is there anything unique about your personal writing process?

Maybe that I have specific, constructed playlists for writing whatever project I'm working on. The chapbook in which "Murder" appears was written almost entirely while listing to dead, gay, male singers such as George Michael, Sylvester, and many others. I also choose specific cocktails for projects and regular work. For example, I've been working on a project where I take business, legal, and other common forms and turn them into poems—when I work on those, I only drink boulevardiers.

How long do you usually spend working on a single poem?

Ten minutes to ten years. Seriously. My poem "A Pile" (*Queen Mob's Teahouse*) was written and revised in about ten minutes. I wrote "Reading Is Fundamental" (*Grist Online*) over ten years and at least sixty drafts.

How long have you been writing poetry? What has changed from your first poem to your newest

work?

Since 1989. My first poem was about an older man I was crushing on and my uncle being diagnosed with HIV. My newest work... Well, not much has changed? Actually, the most recent poem I finished wonders why the aging process prompts us to live more in memory than the present moment.

Who are some of your favorite poets?

Whitman, Rimbaud, Dickinson, Bishop, Eliot, Hughes, Sexton, Merrill, and Ashbery are my classic faves. Rita Dove, Thom Gunn, Sharon Olds, Joe Bolton, Louise Gluck, Mark Doty after that. More currently, Jericho Brown and Randall Mann, along with Khadijah Queen, Franny Choi, Kazumi Chin, Stephen Mills, Ross Gay, Victoria Chang, Todd Dillard, and Jose Hernandez Diaz.

If you had to narrow it down, what three books have had the most impact on your writing?

Syd Field's *Screenplay: The Foundations of Screenwriting*. It makes you think about the work under the wordsmithing no matter what you're writing. *The Man with Night Sweats* by Thom Gunn. Just... Wow. And, this is the weird one, *Sex* by Madonna. That book made me realize you could make a book of and about almost anything with will and resource. I still want to write some wild multi-modal work/collection at some point.

Do you work in any other artistic mediums? If so, how do those other genres inform your poetry?

Fiction, which causes me to always think about the story in my poems and the poems I read, and I wish I gave myself more time to write fiction, although admittedly my fiction is very genre and kooky.

How would you personally define poetry?

Poetry is discovering and enjoying the music housed by and between the words.

Based on your personal experience, what advice would you give to other writers?

Discipline. Poetry does not write and revise itself.

What is the best piece of writing advice you've been given?

Not everyone will like what you do and that's okay.

KAHLOFIED

BRENNAN MCMULLEN

the unibrow and the belly tub, concomitant with butterfly kisses
on the nave, blink into my digestion, it will lead to the heart
i taste most.

the tree of life and the dental appointment with butterfly
drills by candlelight, a tub full of crutches, it will lead to
my pollinated teeth.

the most and "i don't know" rescind a precedence, the ubiquity
of art under running water, your shower thoughts will alleviate
my chewing gums.

the stomata and the mouth whisk, the tallness of a slow burn.
Butterfly flames will untell the stories we leave for
generations.

i don't know how Kahlo inducted us, peering over your shoulder
to see the new bugs and their house plants buried in the jungle.
we are raw and hairy. we are precipicing on germination. we will
bulb like Rivera, like a line drawn between two lines.

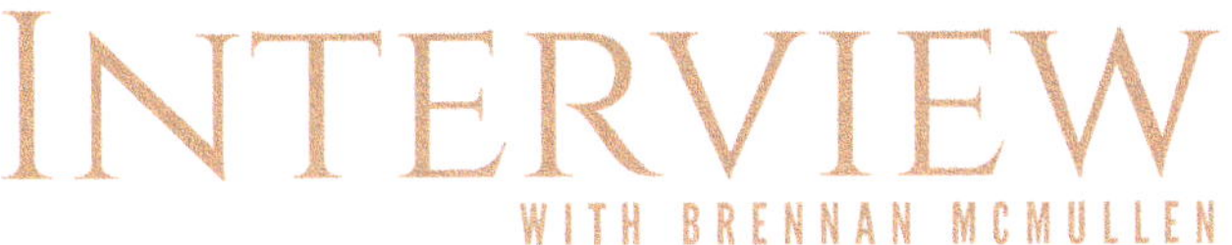

INTERVIEW
WITH BRENNAN MCMULLEN

What inspired the poem?

"Kahlofied" was inspired by the bathroom-sealed belongings of Frida Kahlo, photographed by the esteemed Graciela Iturbide at la Casa Azul. With all her prolificacy, Kahlo endured chronic pain from polio and tragedy. My teeth were grinding while arrested by the crutches in the tub. It took a small resurrection, a butterfly ushering, to move me along from the photograph. Something about Rivera's grief, however, was permanent and left traces of foul pollen on my nerves.

What was the hardest part about writing it?

I tend to avoid writing someone else's story without their consent. This poem was meant to focus on my synesthetic pain. Both the pain of Kahlo's torment and Rivera's neurotic idolatry. Those torturous photographs were a product of Rivera's cache, not Kahlo's place of refuge. To be locked away without the endurance of touch, these items withered in cold tile, despite the many rebirths tolerated by the spirit of Kahlo. I wanted to lean on those crutches after being pulled away.

What is your favorite line from the poem or the line you are most proud of?

"the stomata and the mouth whisk, the tallness of a slow burn," speaks to the guard cells of a plant epidermis, the bathroom tooth cleaning utensil, and a long wicked candle. Together, I imagine the brushing of butterfly wings against the stem of the flower as it finds its way to sustenance. But it is a challenge for the weak-winged. It is also that intimate mirror moment when you clean the rot out of your gums for a few minutes in the face of your reflection, stepping up to your weaknesses. For Kahlo, it must have been difficult, back braced and armpits screaming. Reaching for a mouth while one's wings are pinching. The wick of one's stamina ashing. Every moment in that bathroom is guarded, shielding the world from untold suffering. A cleaning climb that does well for the stem, but strains the Lepidoptera. Kahlo's body is the plant, and her spirit is in flight.

Who are some of your favorite poets?

First to mind are Terrance Hayes, Zachary Schomburg, Anne Sexton, and Max Rtivo. I also really enjoy Bianca Stone, Krysten Hill, Dominique Christina, Denise Frohman, Morgan Parker, Bill Knott, Anne Carson, Solmaz Sharif, and James Tate. And a few budding poets I expect will be well known soon: Shivani Singh, Ali Larew, Jason Chin, and Kristina Saliba.

If you had to narrow it down, what three books have had the most impact on your writing?

Nochita by Dia Felix, *The Museum of Eterna's Novel (The First Good Novel)* by Macedonio Fernandez, and *The Orange Eats Creeps* by Grace Krilanovich. I go to these books when I'm sick of writing and need to be sicker.

How would you personally define poetry?

Urban planning alone in a desert and all the maps are drawn in the sand. It isn't until you cower like a powerful bird and bury your head beneath the earth that you see the city has been built in hypogeal structures, and a hard working cab driver nearly decapitates half your skull.

Caress the Contours of the Ditch

WREN HANKS

In the dream he   invites me for a tryst in the men's bathroom anyway
Holds the door open for me
          caress the contours of the ditch   my friend asks how I knew
          the voices were all mine
The door he opened led to diner seats
What kind of man are you when everyone   has been so nice
a transgender register   of secrets pill-thick
          caress the contours of the ditch   my friend asks how I knew
          he'd bend me over only in   the safety of my own mind
The door he opened led to a deep freezer
The door he opened led to a plate of fries   I fell in love with them
          Opened my mouth like a ditch
I ate them all he said   *Oh no, I need you closer*

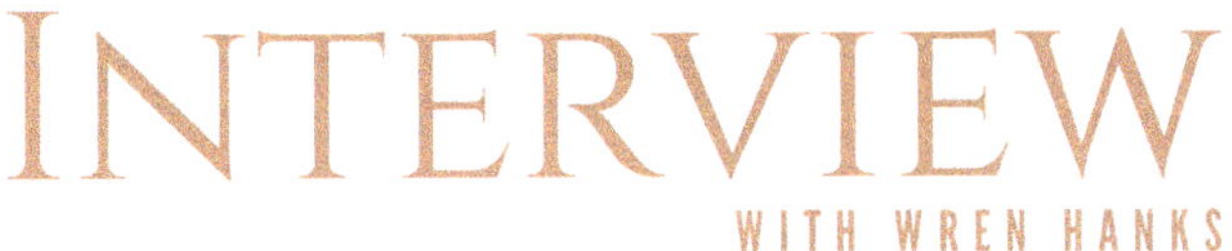

INTERVIEW

WITH WREN HANKS

What inspired the poem?

This poem is from a series of pieces from my new chapbook manuscript, *Lily-livered*, that deal with memory, PTSD/assault, and cycles of trauma and harm in queer communities. It was inspired by a diner that's been a backdrop in several of my dreams. It's the last poem in the series and builds on lines and imagery that occur in the previous poems, specifically on the concept of a "ditch" as a place where painful memories converge and elide.

How much revision went into this poem?

Because I'd built a fair amount of scaffolding for this series in earlier poems, I began this piece knowing roughly where I wanted to end up. As a result, "Caress the Contours of the Ditch" didn't require months of revision like some of the other pieces in *Lily-livered* did. It took me a few drafts to settle on the format (giving my work space to breathe on the page isn't always intuitive for me—sometimes it feels like I'm cracking open the poem's ribs), but the individual lines survived virtually unchanged from the initial draft.

Is this poem categorical of your work? Why or why not?

I think this poem is pretty categorical of my work. I often get stuck in rituals of repetition, which I think of as casting a spell in the sense that repeating words / phrases sets an intention. As a trans person, I'm interested in the line as a body can be remade (over and over) and what reactions those shifts evoke in a reader. I think slippage tends to be comfortable for queer and trans writers in the way it's not necessarily for cis, straight ones. The way definitions change inside the poem, in ways I can't always predict, is one of the most exciting parts of writing for me.

What is your favorite line from the poem or the line you are most proud of?

My favorite pair of lines is, "The door he opened led to a plate of fries / I fell in love with them."

Is there anything unique about your personal writing process?

My writing process is usually research-based, and I tend to obsess over a single topic for several years! For instance, right now I am working on a project about St. Francis, so I have been reading/watching materials related to *The Little Flowers of St. Francis*, lay Franciscans, and the American Christian left.

How long do you usually spend working on a single poem?

It varies, but I usually spend at least a month on a short poem; often, longer poems take upwards of six months.

Who are some of your favorite poets?

William Blake, Feng Sun Chen, Natalie Eilbert, Eric Baus, Elizabeth Bishop, Cyrée Jarelle Johnson, Richard Siken—honestly, it's a long list!

Where can readers find more of your work?

My apocalypse chapbook, *Prophet Fever*, is sold out, but you can find *The Rise of Genderqueer* (*Brain Mill Press*, 2018) for sale at the publisher's website. I also have recent work in *DIAGRAM*, *Indiana Review*, and *New South*.

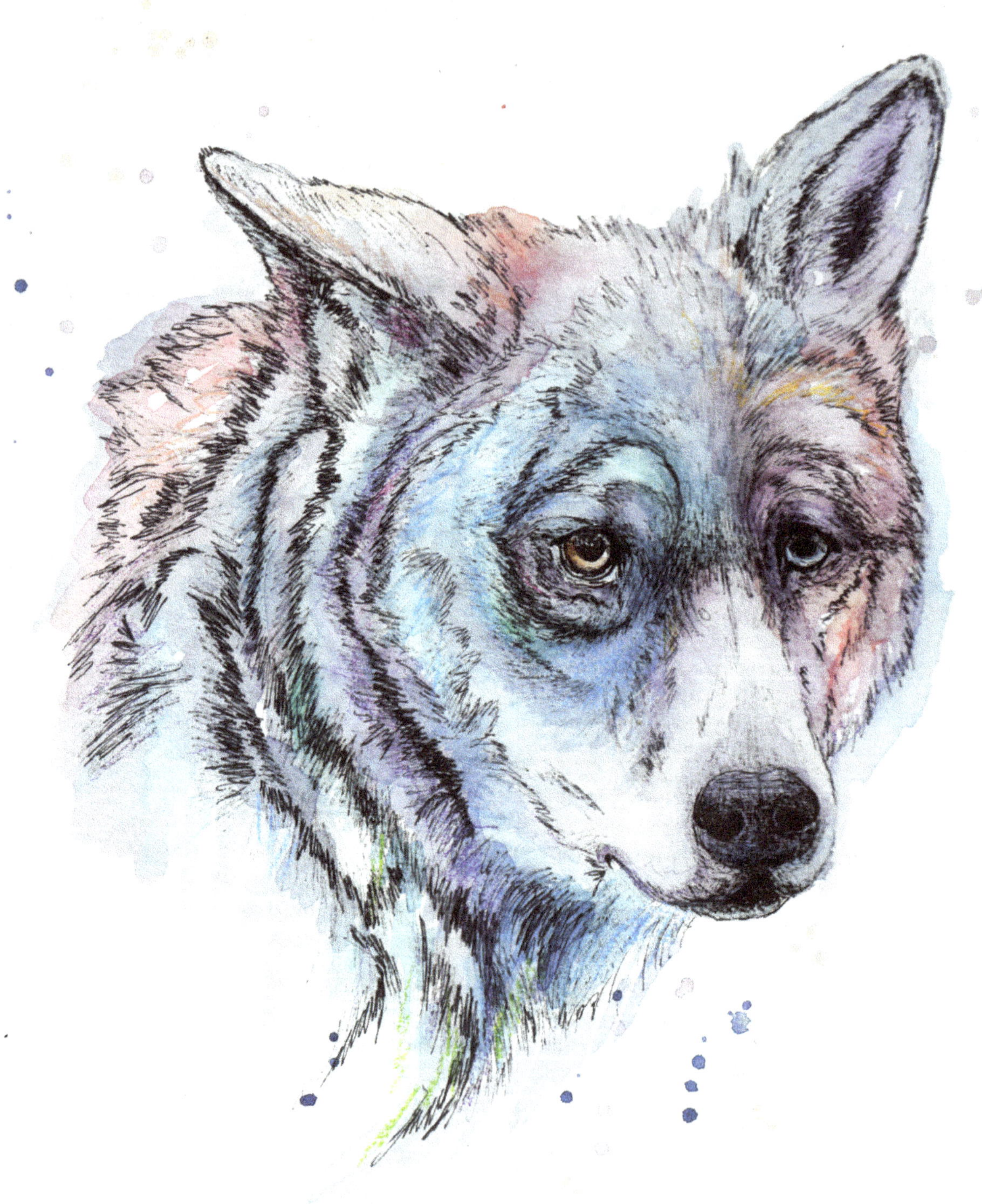

KELSEY M. EVANS'
WOLF

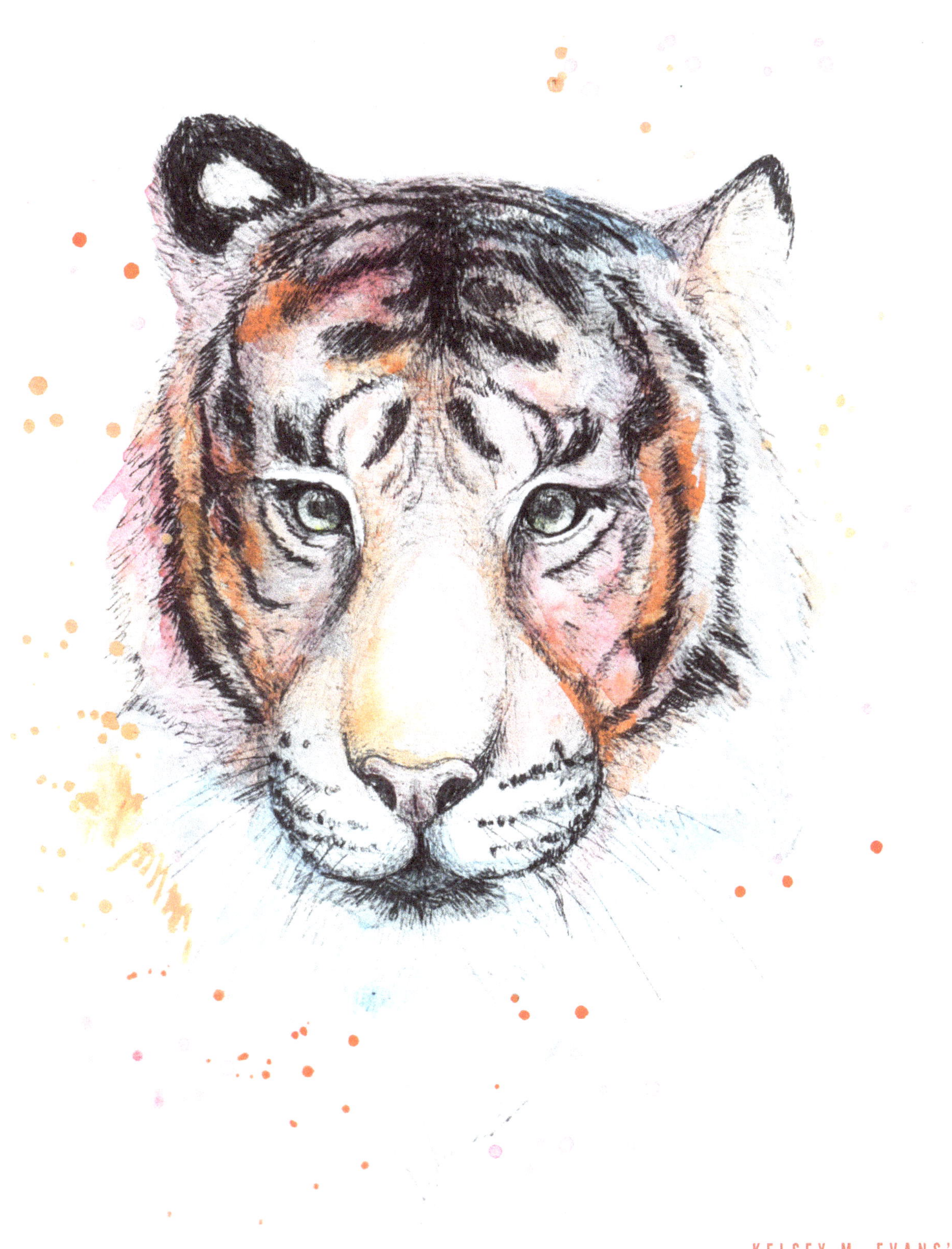

KELSEY M. EVANS'
TIGER

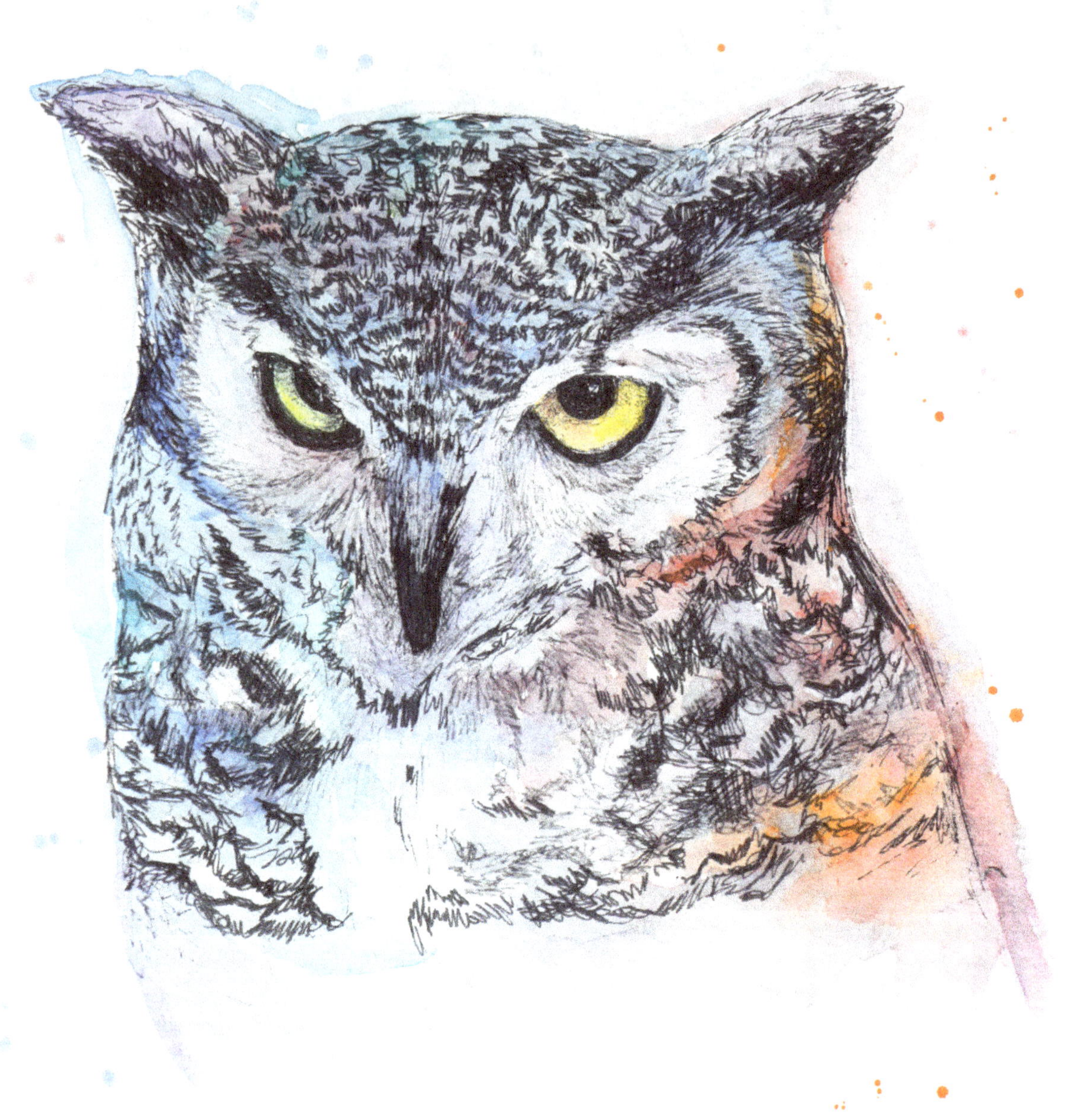

KELSEY M. EVANS'
OWL

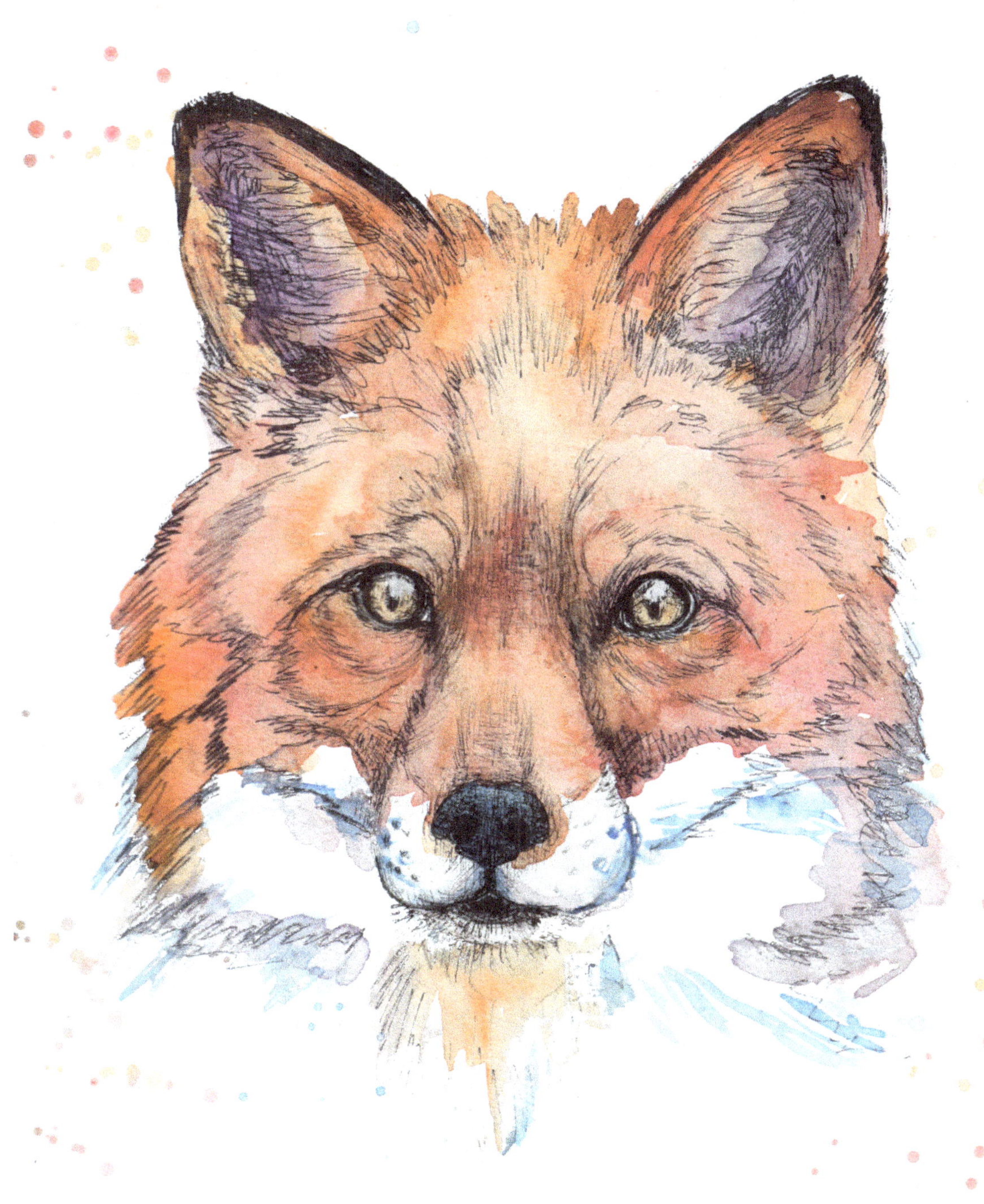

KELSEY M. EVANS'
FOX

QUESTIONS AND ANSWERS

A
GRAPHIC POEM
BY
JAKE GOLDWASSER

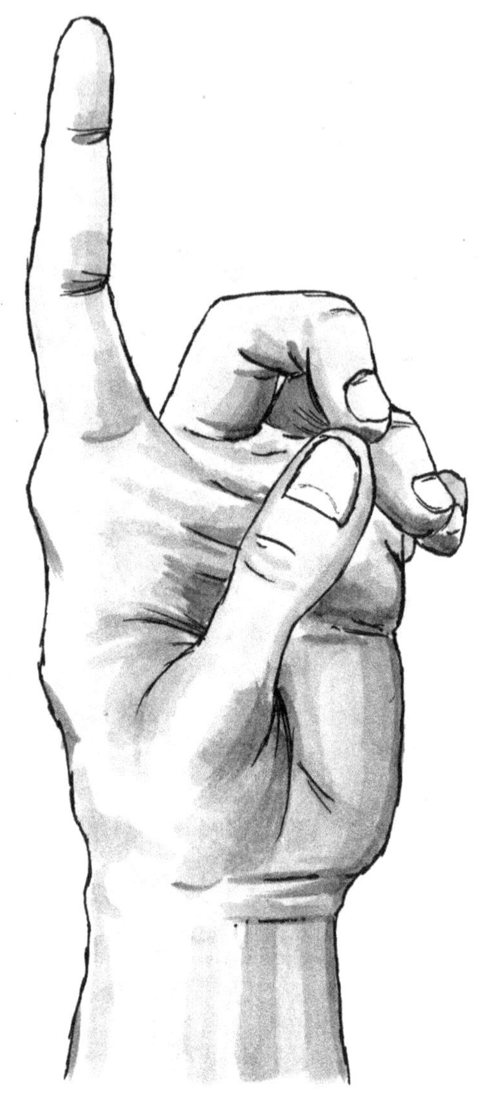

QUESTIONS

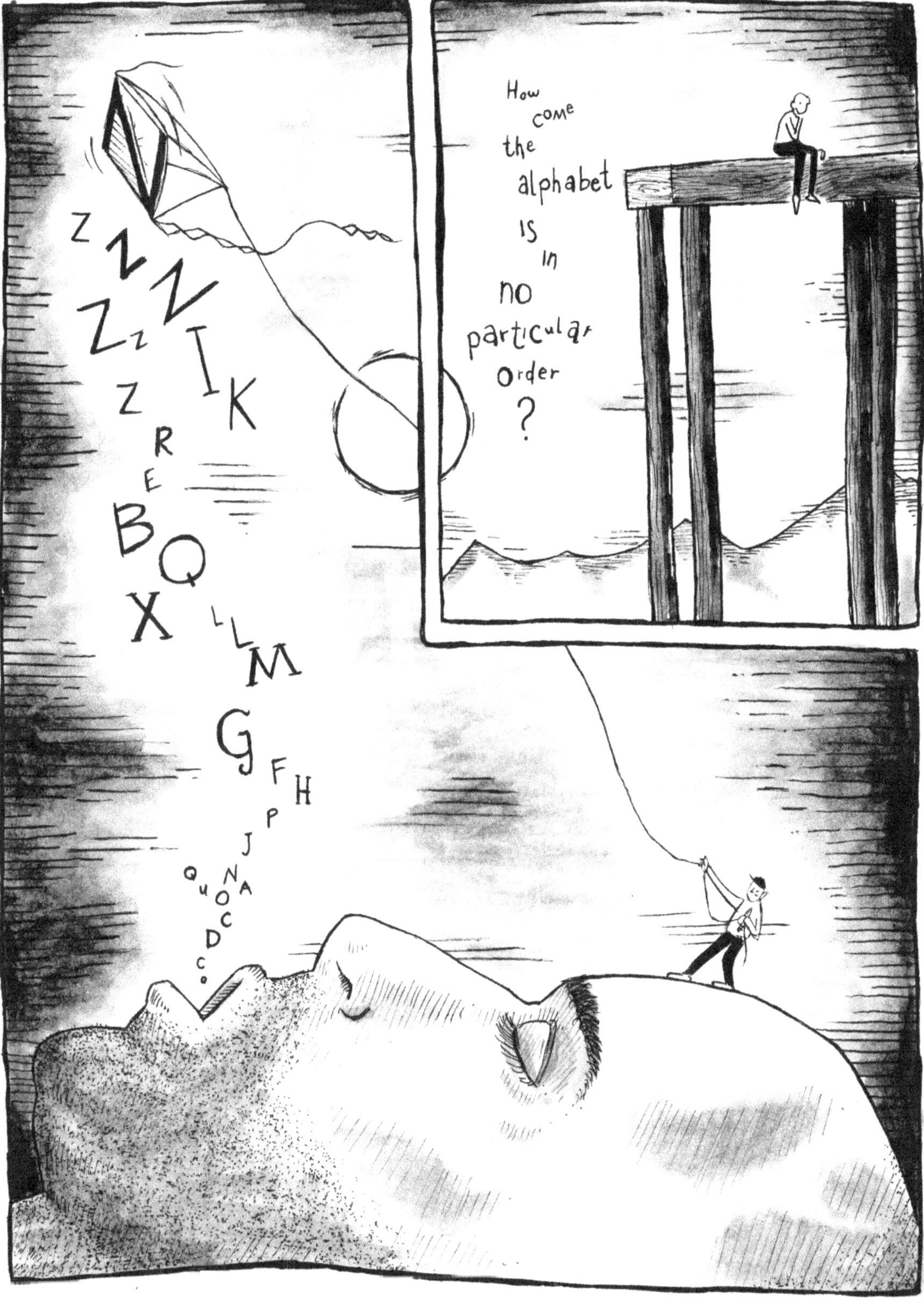
How come the alphabet is in no particular order ?

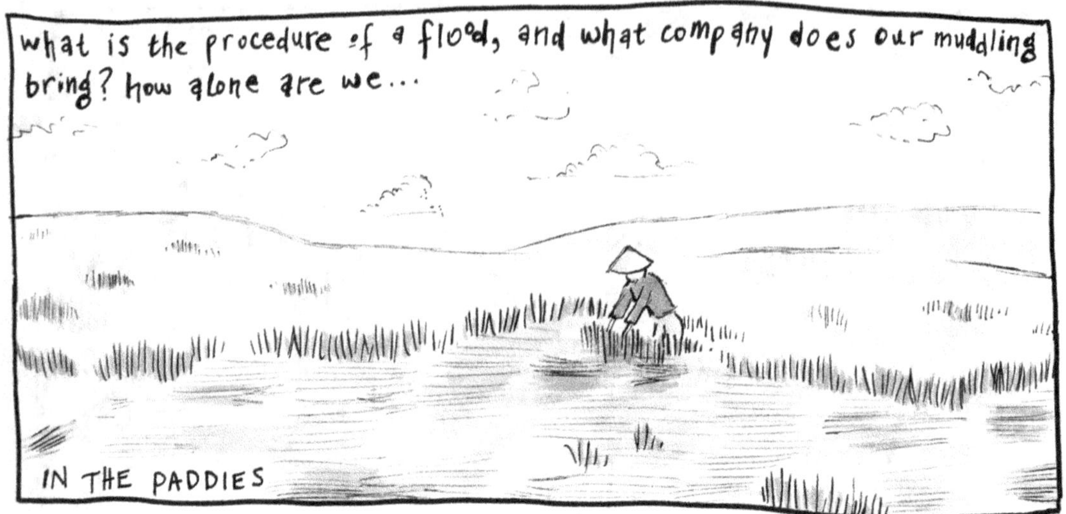
what is the procedure of a flood, and what company does our muddling bring? how alone are we...
IN THE PADDIES

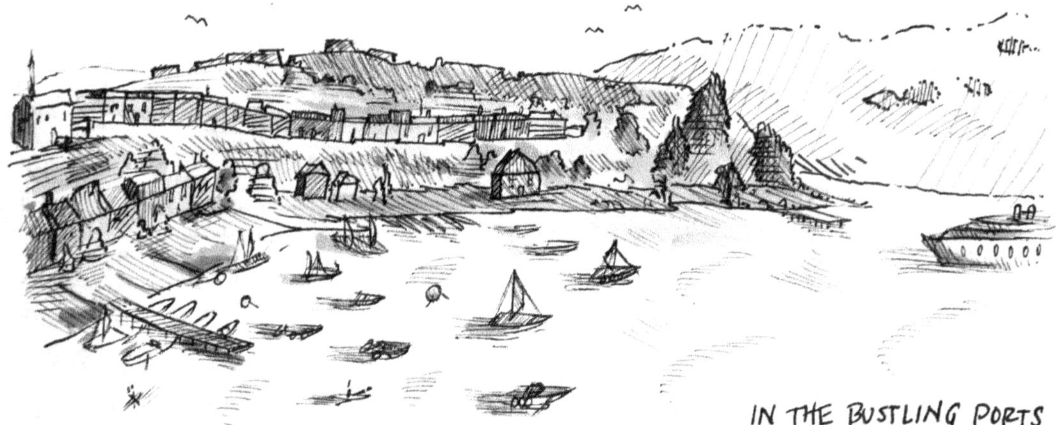
IN THE BUSTLING PORTS

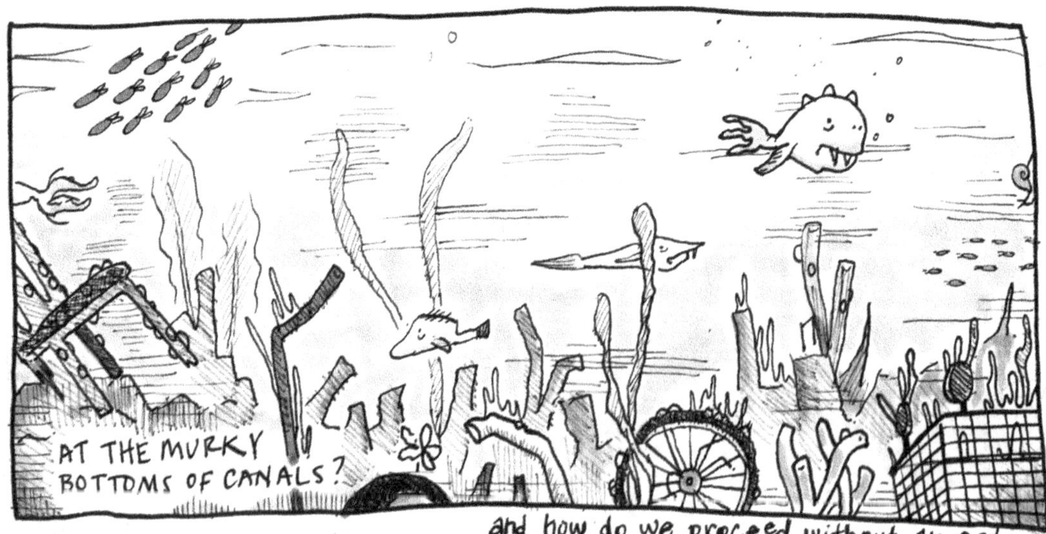
AT THE MURKY BOTTOMS OF CANALS?
and how do we proceed without an order?

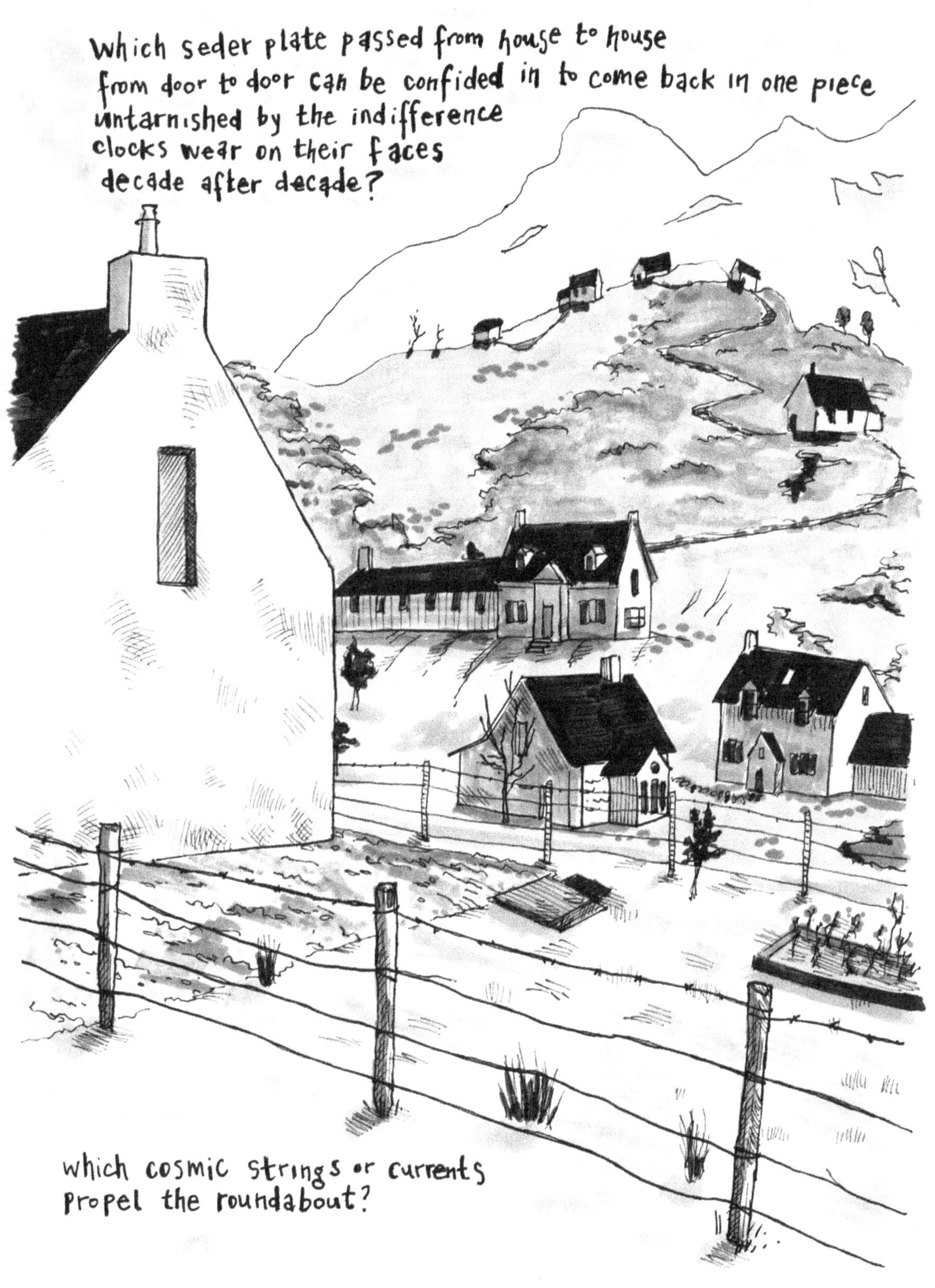
Which seder plate passed from house to house
from door to door can be confided in to come back in one piece
untarnished by the indifference
clocks wear on their faces
decade after decade?
which cosmic strings or currents
propel the roundabout?

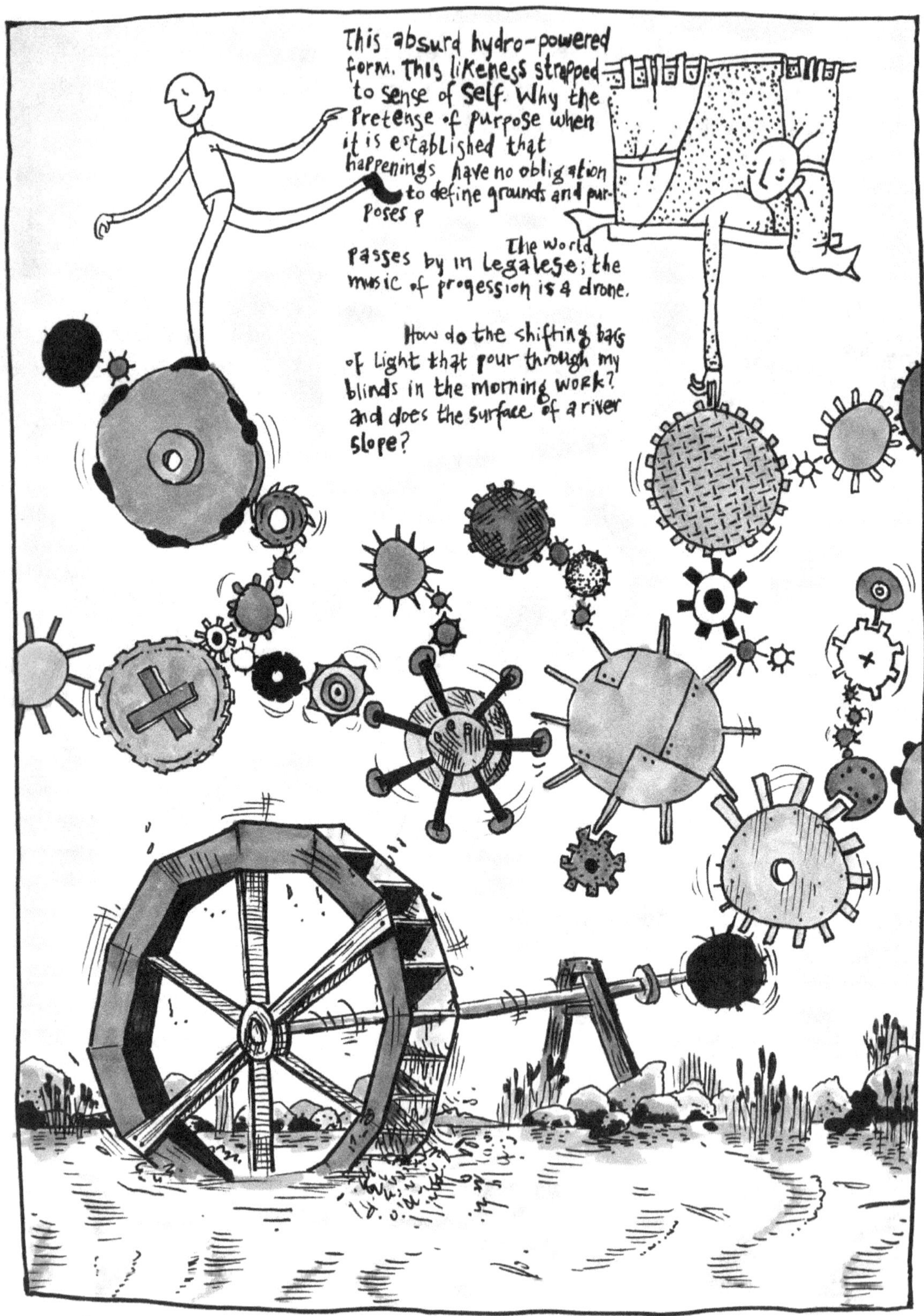
This absurd hydro-powered form. This likeness strapped to sense of SELF. Why the pretense of purpose when it is established that happenings have no obligation to define grounds and purposes?
The world passes by in legalese; the music of progession is a drone.
How do the shifting bars of light that pour through my blinds in the morning work? and does the surface of a river slope?

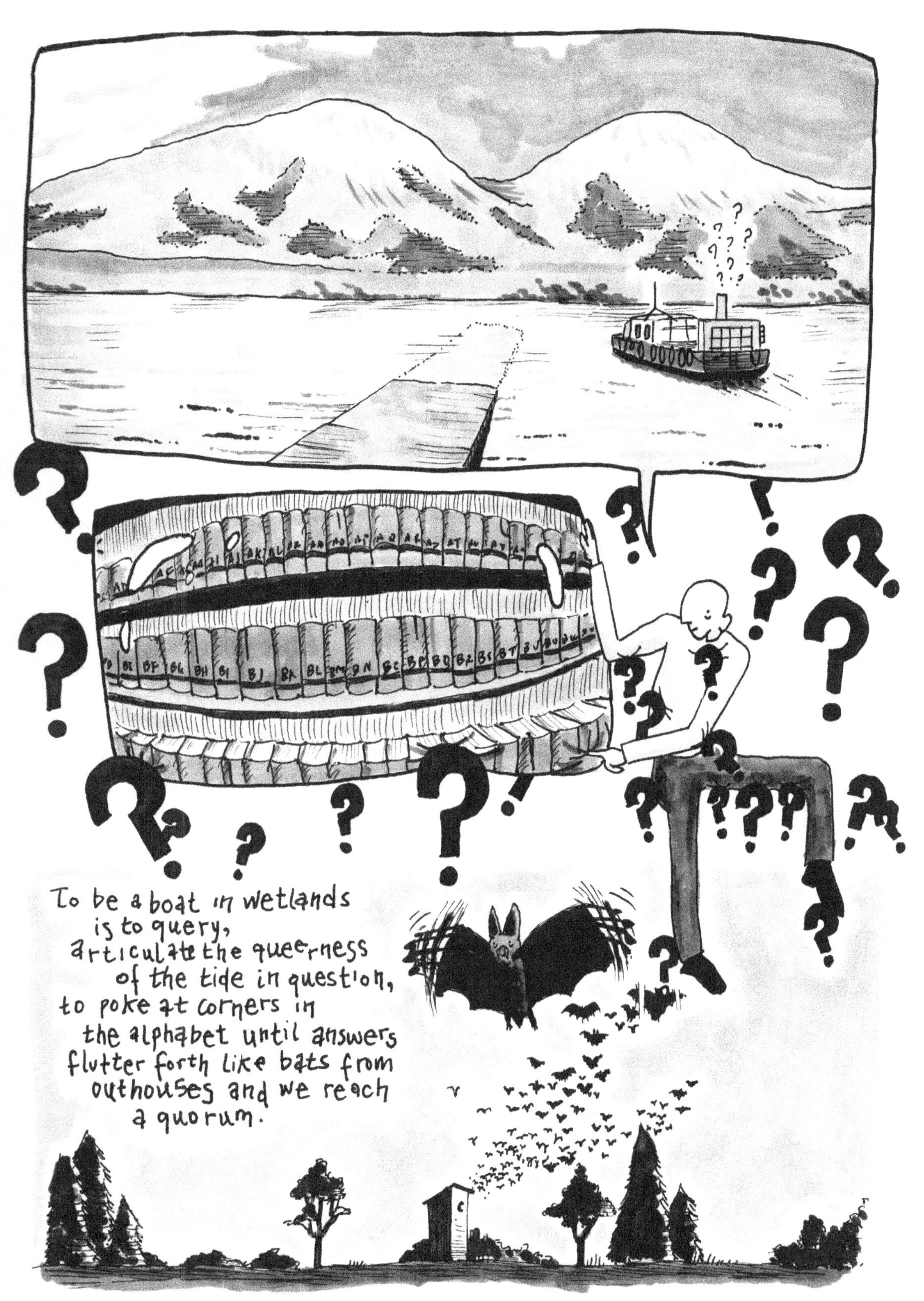
To be a boat in wetlands
is to query,
articulate the queerness
of the tide in question,
to poke at corners in
the alphabet until answers
flutter forth like bats from
outhouses and we reach
a quorum.

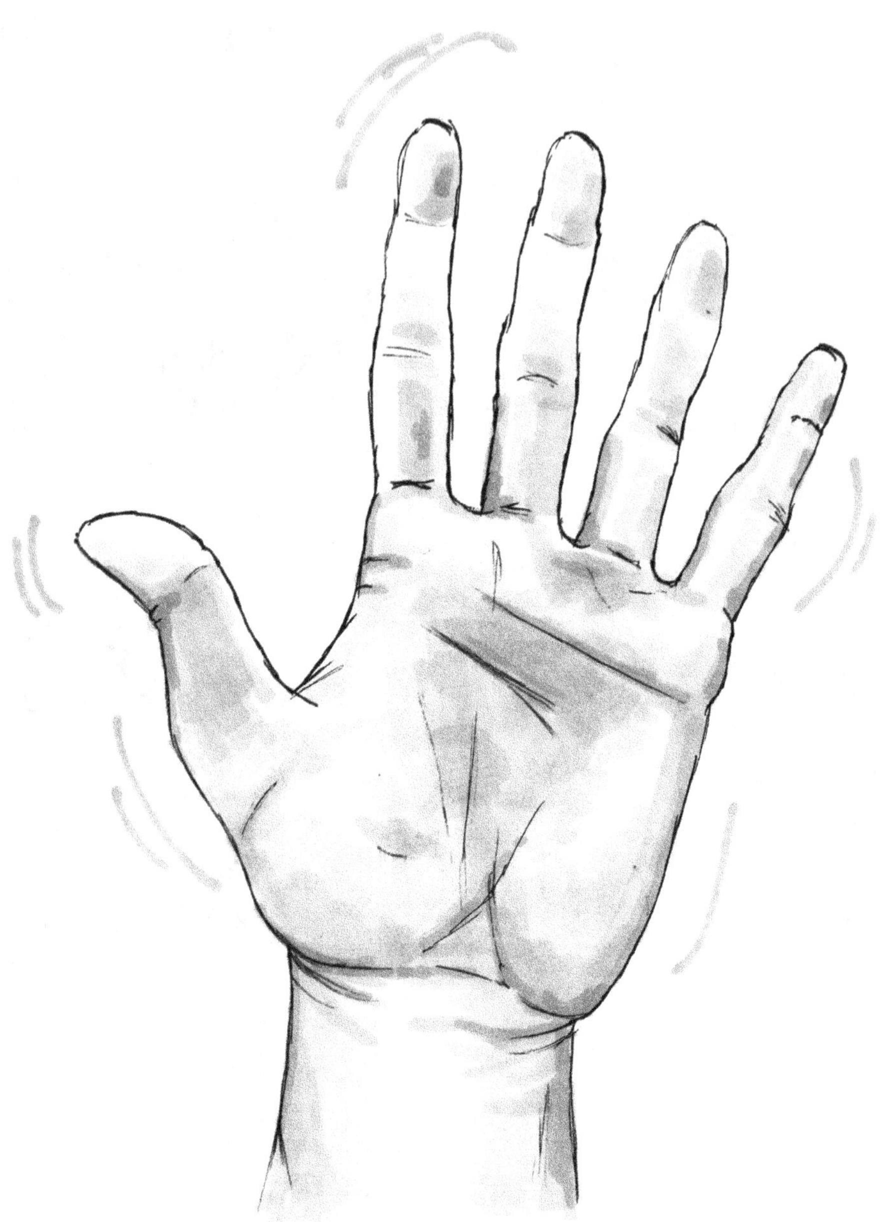

ANSWERS

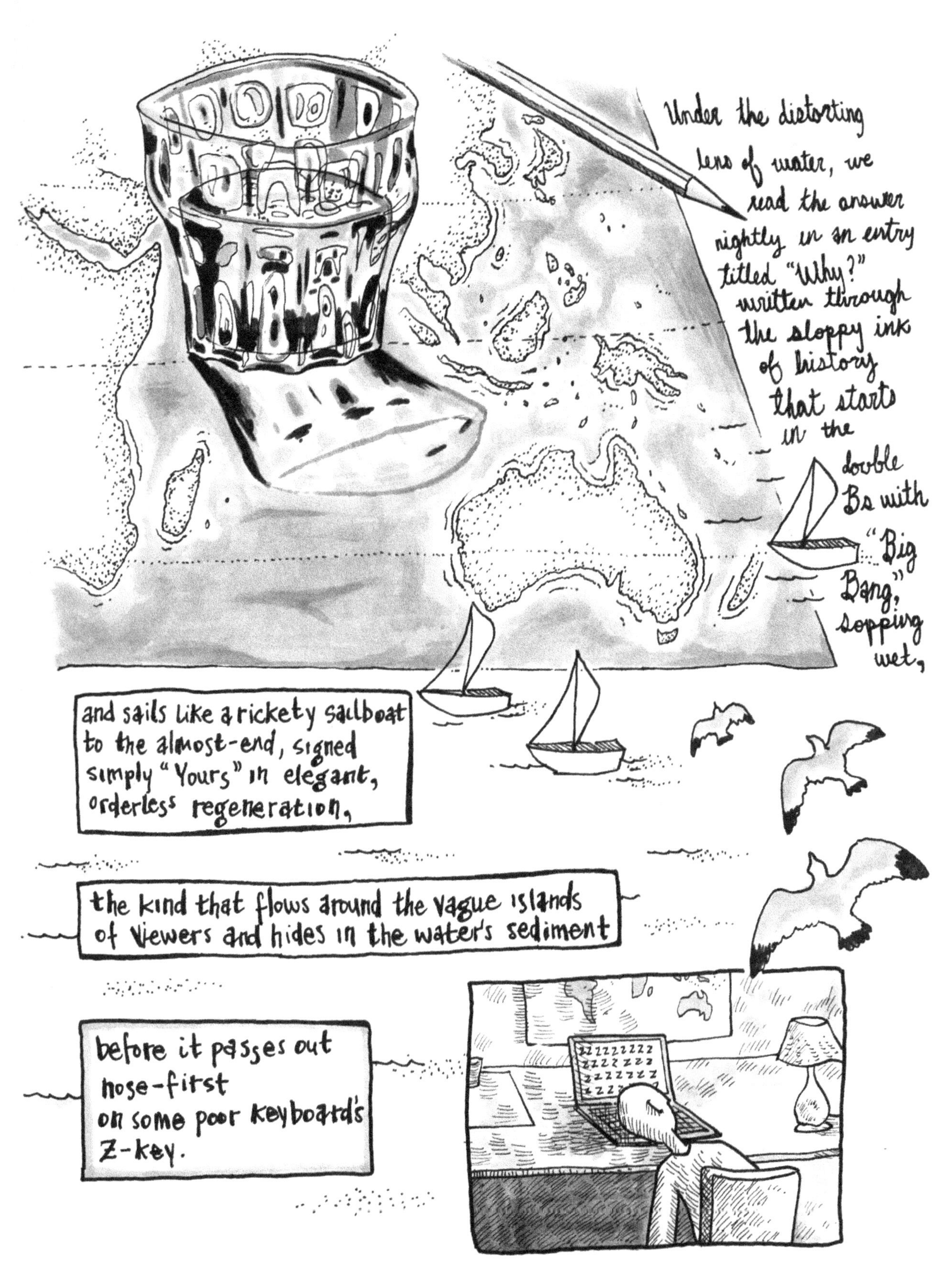
Under the distorting lens of water, we read the answer nightly in an entry titled "Why?" written through the sloppy ink of history that starts in the double Bs with "Big Bang," sopping wet,
and sails like a rickety sailboat to the almost-end, signed simply "Yours" in elegant, orderless regeneration,
the kind that flows around the vague islands of viewers and hides in the water's sediment
before it passes out nose-first on some poor keyboard's Z-key.
zzzzzzz
zzzzzzz
zzzzzzz
zzz

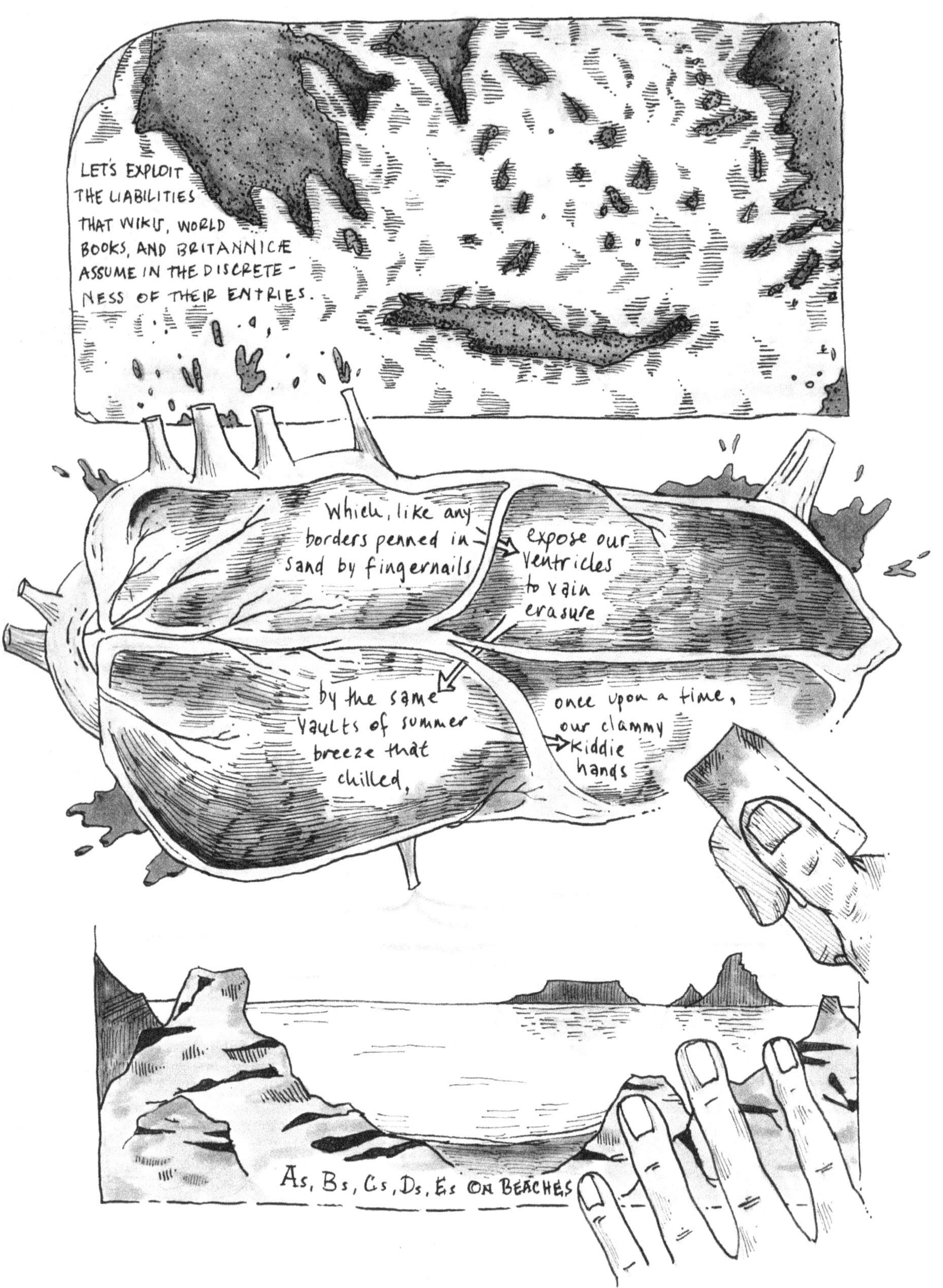
LET'S EXPLOIT THE LIABILITIES THAT WIKIS, WORLD BOOKS, AND BRITANNICÆ ASSUME IN THE DISCRETENESS OF THEIR ENTRIES.
Which, like any borders penned in sand by fingernails
expose our ventricles to vain erasure
by the same vaults of summer breeze that chilled,
once upon a time, our clammy kiddie hands
As, Bs, Cs, Ds, Es ON BEACHES

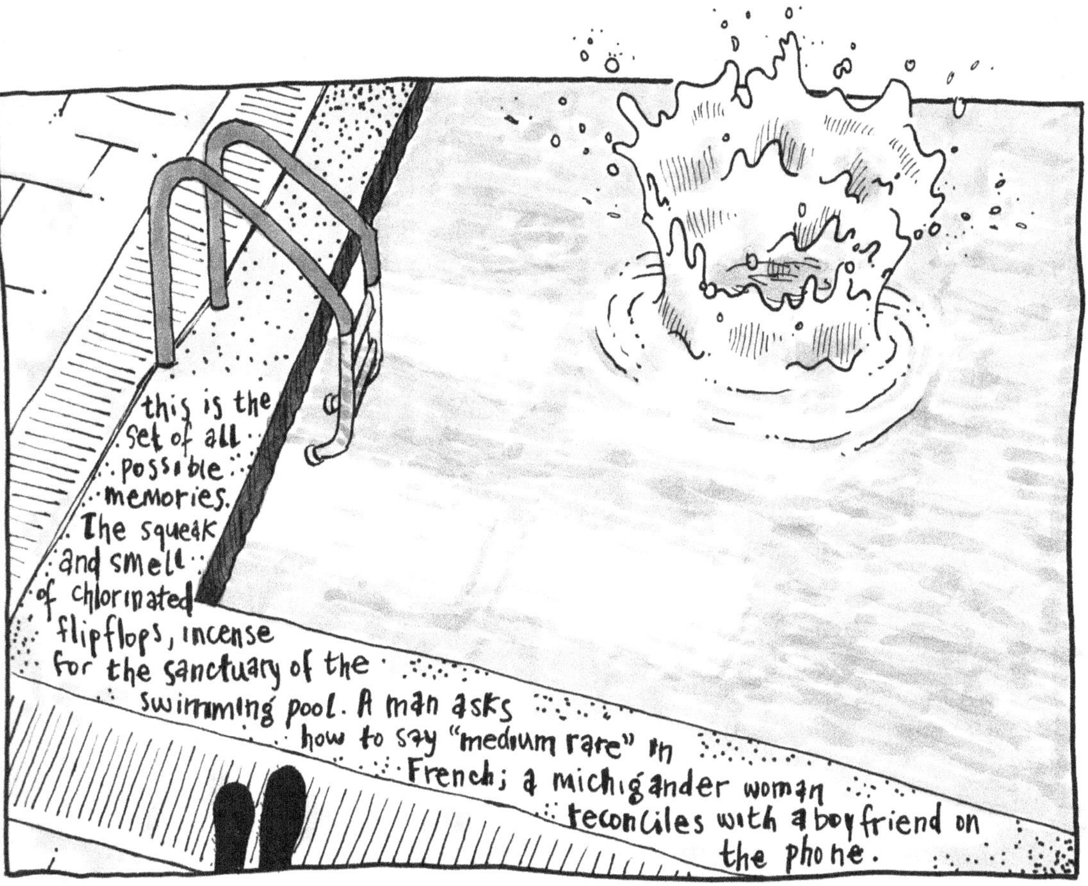

this is the set of all possible memories. The squeak and smell of chlorinated flipflops, incense for the sanctuary of the swimming pool. A man asks how to say "medium rare" in French; a michigander woman reconciles with a boyfriend on the phone.

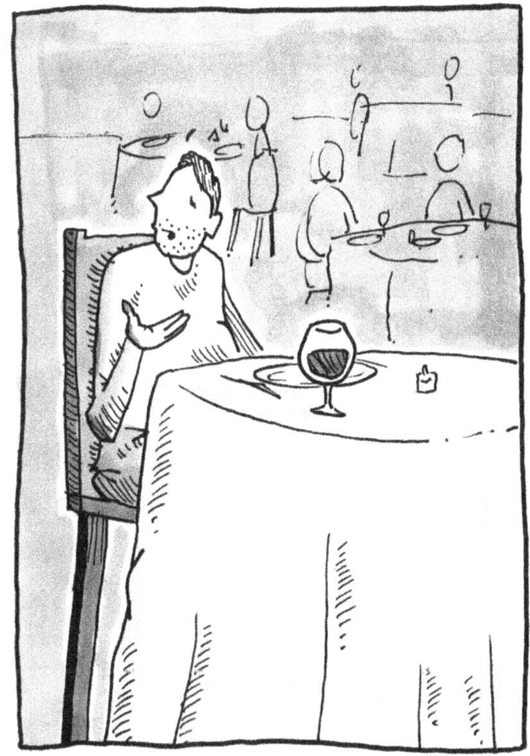

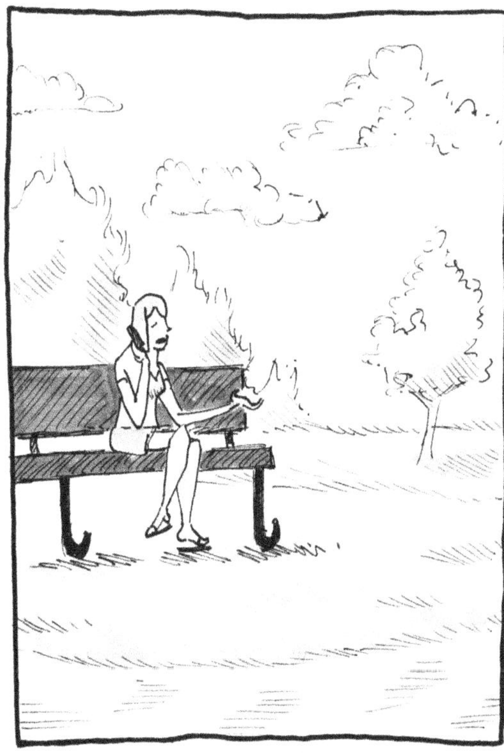

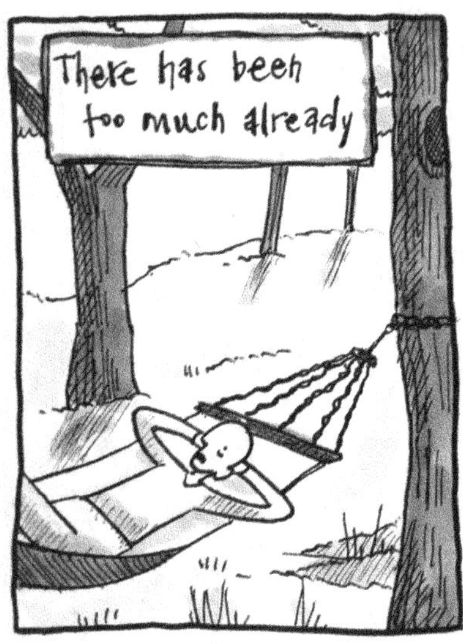
There has been too much already

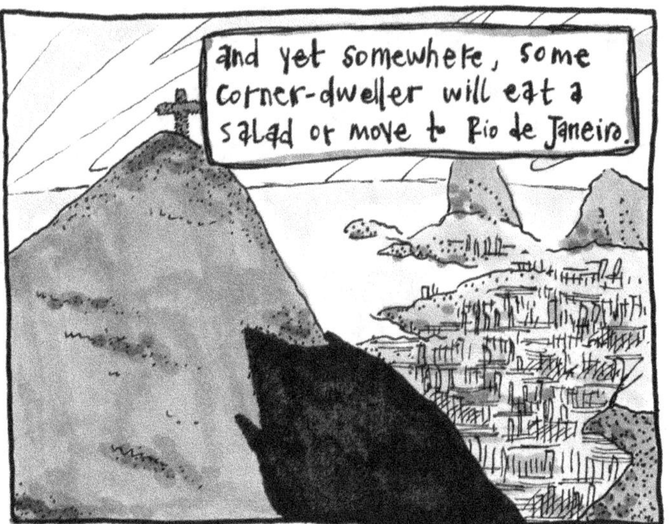
and yet somewhere, some corner-dweller will eat a salad or move to Rio de Janeiro.

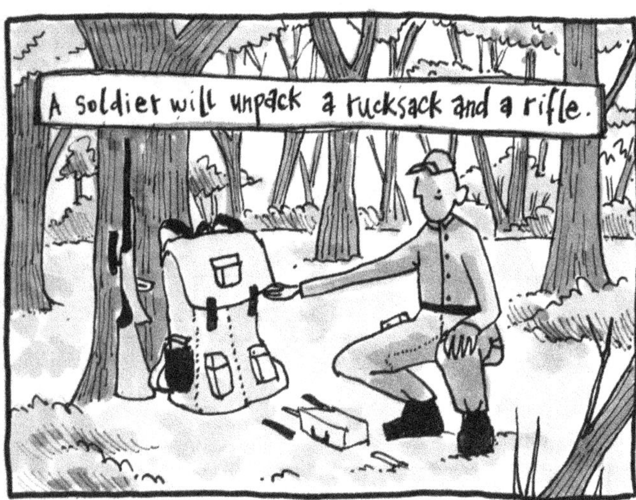
A soldier will unpack a rucksack and a rifle.

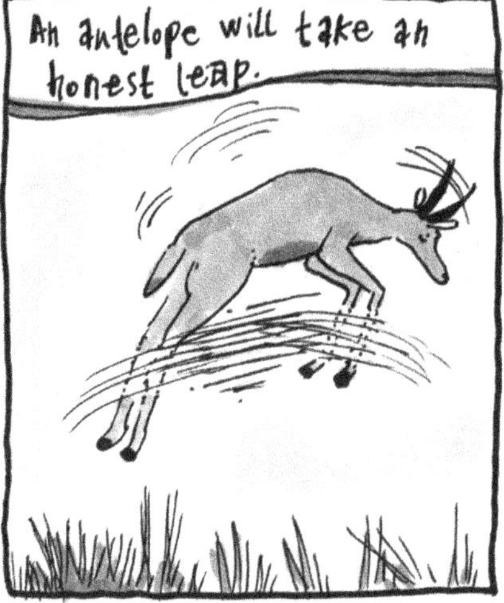
An antelope will take an honest leap.

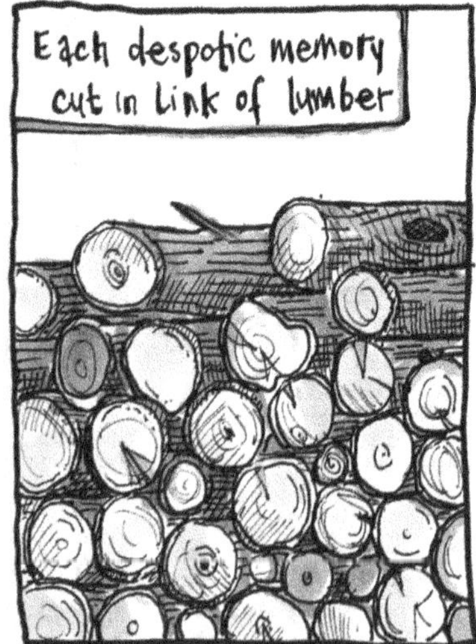
Each despotic memory cut in link of lumber

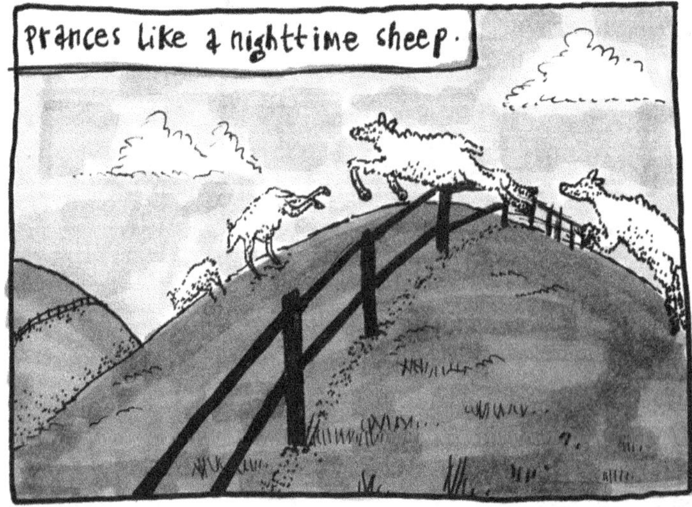
Prances like a nighttime sheep.

this is where the entries swim in one school without starts or ends.

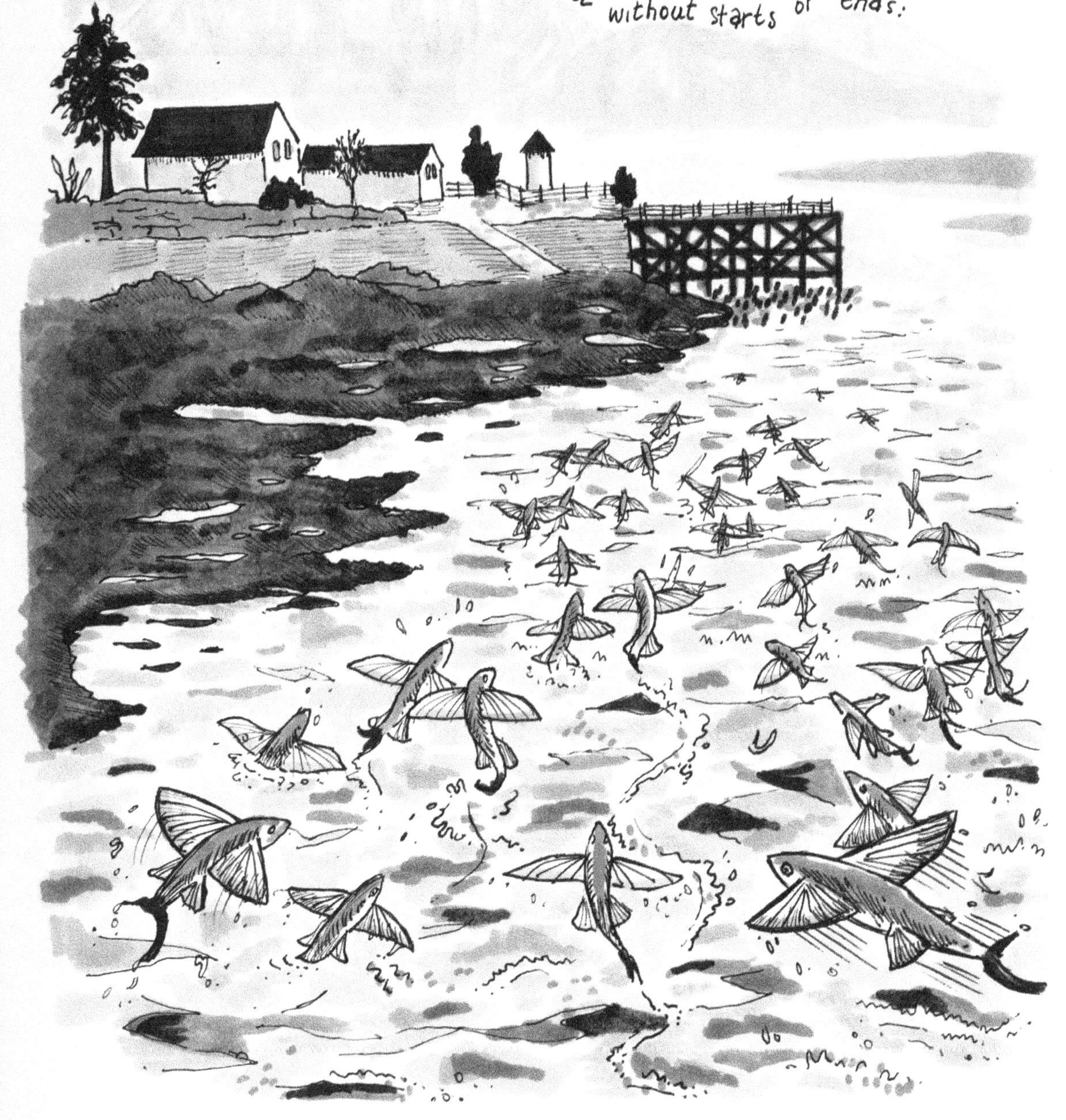

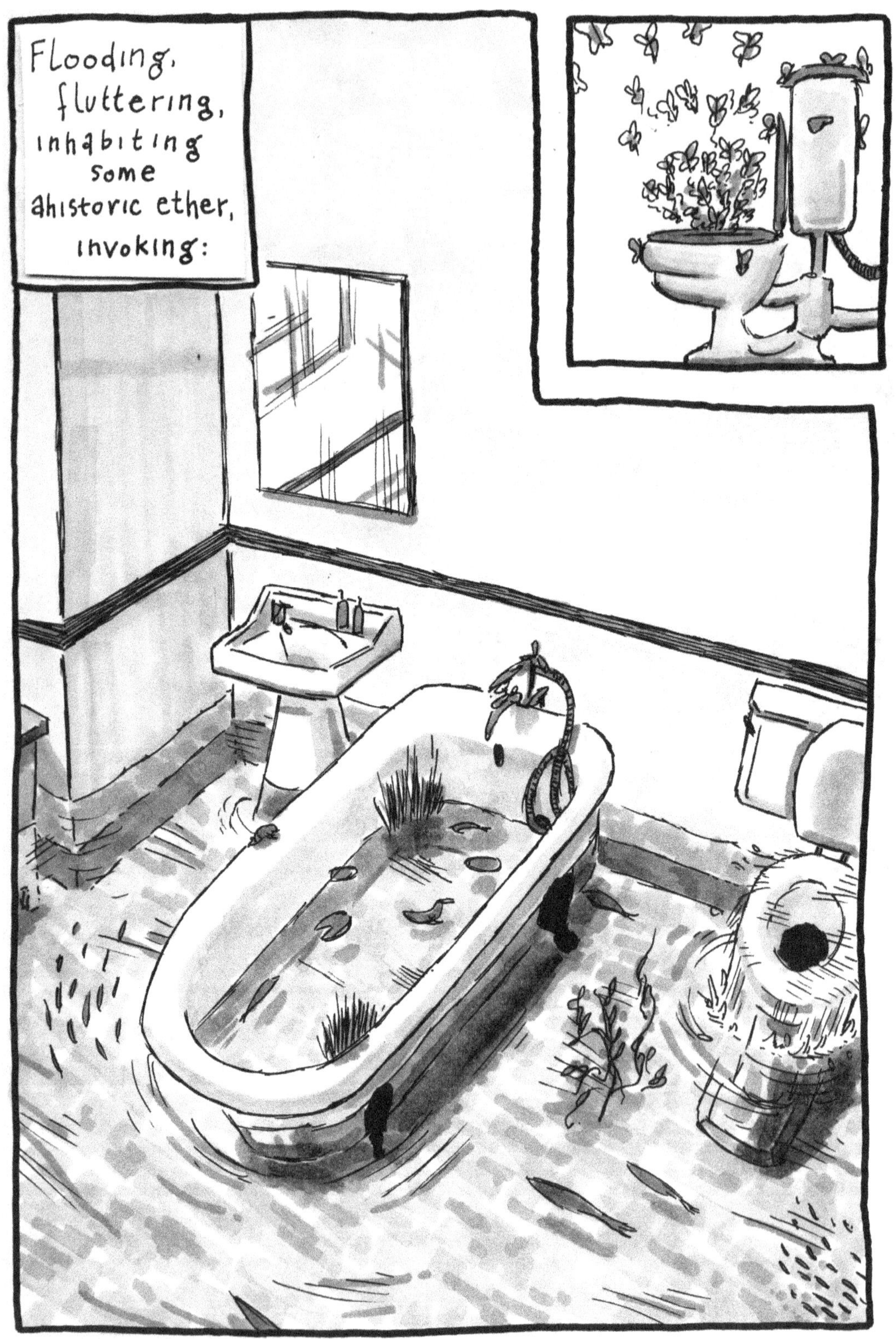
Flooding,
fluttering,
inhabiting
some
ahistoric ether,
invoking:

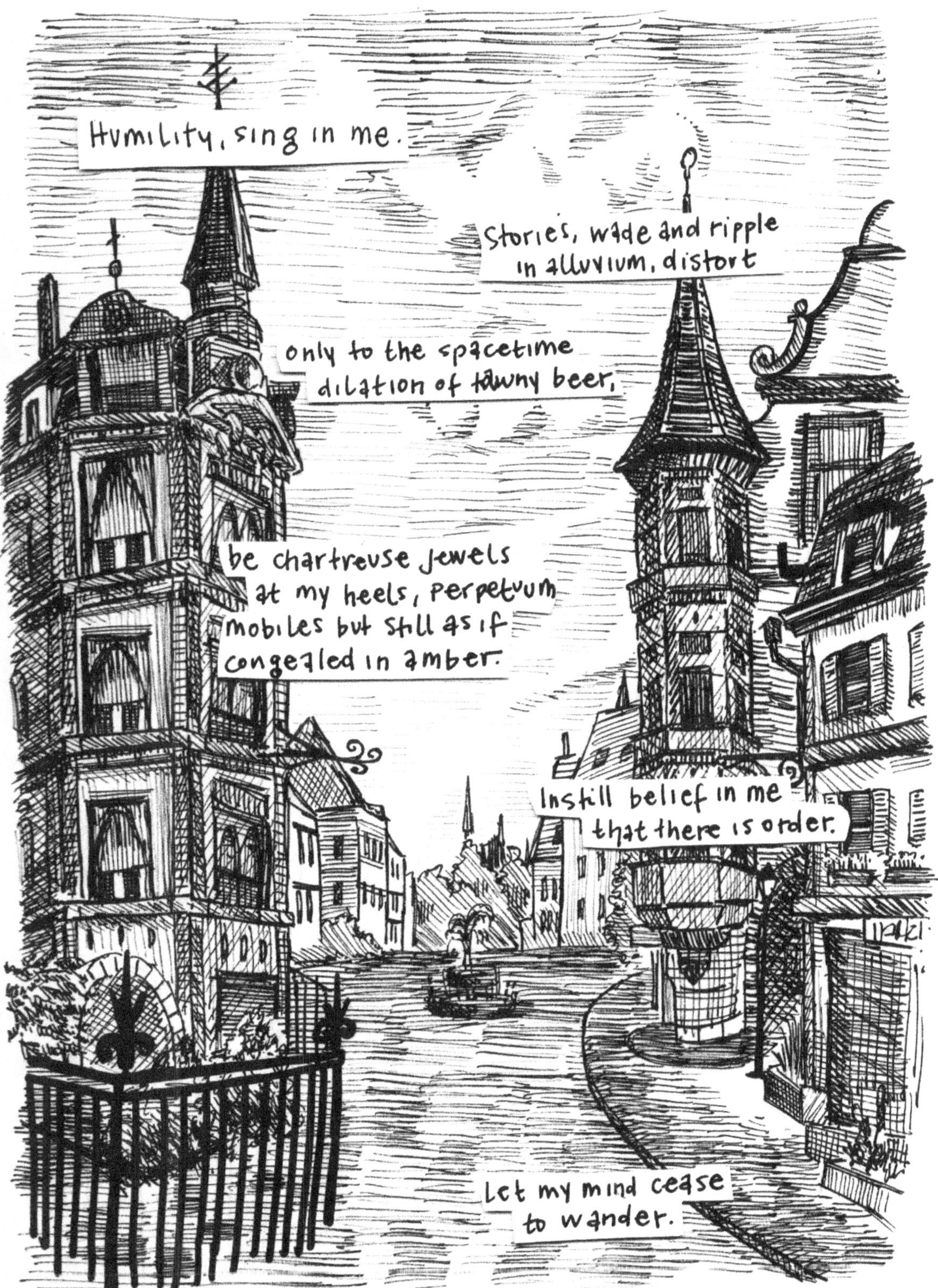
Humility, sing in me.
Stories, wade and ripple in alluvium, distort
only to the spacetime dilation of tawny beer,
be chartreuse jewels at my heels, perpetuum mobiles but still as if congealed in amber.
Instill belief in me that there is order.
Let my mind cease to wander.

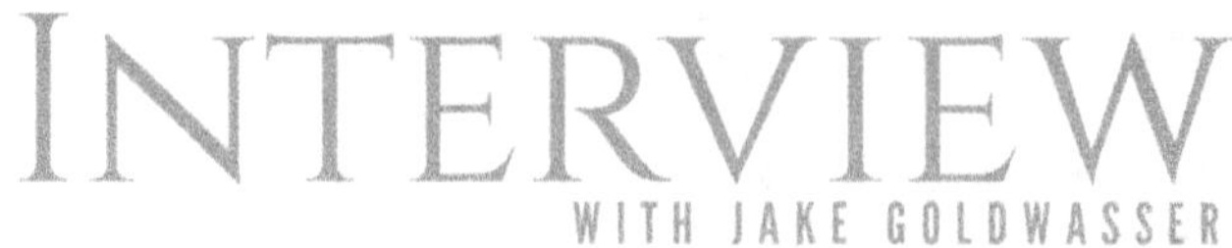

INTERVIEW
WITH JAKE GOLDWASSER

Did you have a difficult time deciding on whether to add a title to your work?

Titles have always been a favorite part of the process for me, and I have many, many titles that I haven't gotten around to acting on (yet!). In particular, I had a few working titles for this piece. The main one was "Encyclopedia in No Particular Order," which I hope to repurpose sometime.

When did you create "Questions and Answers"?

I wrote "Questions and Answers" in San Francisco before and after the 2016 election, and I illustrated it while working on various farms in the UK in 2018. Most of the images are real things I saw while in the UK. Around the time of the election, I had a vision of a flood myth for modern times. There is of course the threat of literal flood due to climate change, but there is also a flood of information, of outrage, of experience, and a million other things, which I allude to in the work.

This comic moves effortlessly through different paneling structures, from traditional box panels to looser blends of text and image. Were these organizational choices mapped out in advance or realized during the drawing phase?

I'm not particularly good at planning anything out before the drawing phase. Drawing is a kind of reasoning, just like writing is, and some visual ideas need to be worked out during the drawing process. The panels are part and parcel of the illustrations, and so I came up with the paneling structure when I made my first drafts of the illustrations.

How early in the creation or planning of this comic did you land on the "Questions and Answers" section breaks?

This piece was originally about seventy pages long, cut down to about a quarter of that. I completely reordered the work in that process, but the question-and-answer format emerged early in the writing process. I'm realizing it mirrors this interview format nicely as well!

Was there any theme or idea you hoped to address with this work?

I was hoping to present a world that I see as very disorderly and disjointed by using a disorderly and disjointed comic structure—no table of contents or neat, linear plot. Only vague questions and vague answers. This has always been the way my own mind has worked, and it has always been a frustration I've had with the way institutions and publications are structured. I have a hard time reading books in order. I like to "ricochet," as Billy Collins once put it, between works of art, ideas, disciplines, etc. I wanted to make a comic that communicated that.

What instruments did you use here?

I used copic pens and copic alcohol-based markers on bristol board, for the most part. They were a convenient medium because I was traveling at the time, but when I'm home, I prefer old-school dip pens.

Transitioning from creating artwork to fully-fledged comics can often feel daunting for artists. Do you have any tips for aspiring comic writers? What were things you wish you would have known when you were starting out?

Developing a process can't be done a priori—like almost everything, you need to build a process by taking on a big project. Congratulate yourself every time you make a mistake. The bigger the better.

If you had to narrow it down, who would you say are your three biggest influences?

The English illustrator Quentin Blake, the Irish poet Seamus Heaney, and the American cartoonist Roz Chast.

What other mediums have influenced your work? How?

I often think of comics in terms of film — especially since many people aren't familiar with literary comics but are familiar with movies. Cinematography in particular is a helpful analogy. Where you put the camera really changes the story.

What are your own artistic goals for the future? Simply, what do you want to do next?

I want to publish a graphic novel. Specifically, I want to write a book about the absurdity of social status, how normal it is to tank one's well-being to secure prestige. I just need to find the right story to tackle that subject.

Where can our readers find more of your work? Have you been published before?

Yes! You can find my cartoon work in *The New Yorker* and *Weekly Humorist*, and you can find my poetry in various places listed on my website (jacobgoldwasser.com). I also have an Instagram (@jakegoldwasser).

Paper Menu

Kat Y. Tang

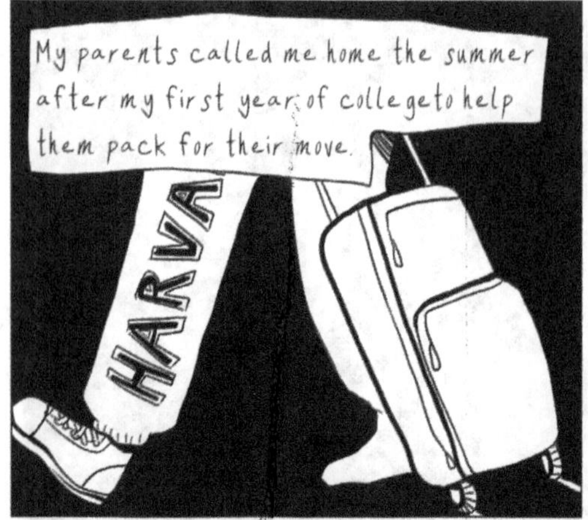
My parents called me home the summer after my first year of college to help them pack for their move.
HARVA

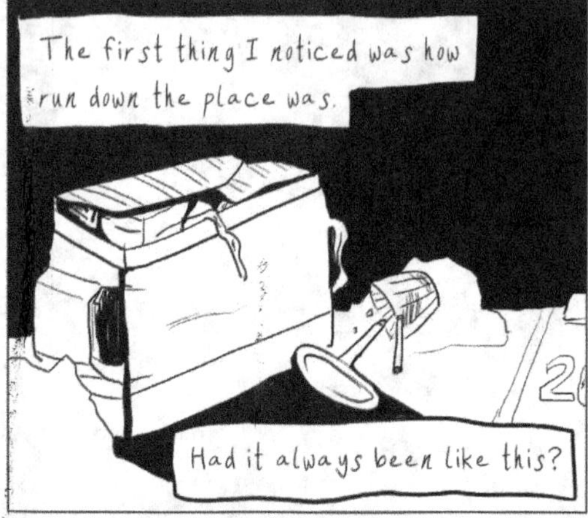
The first thing I noticed was how run down the place was.
Had it always been like this?

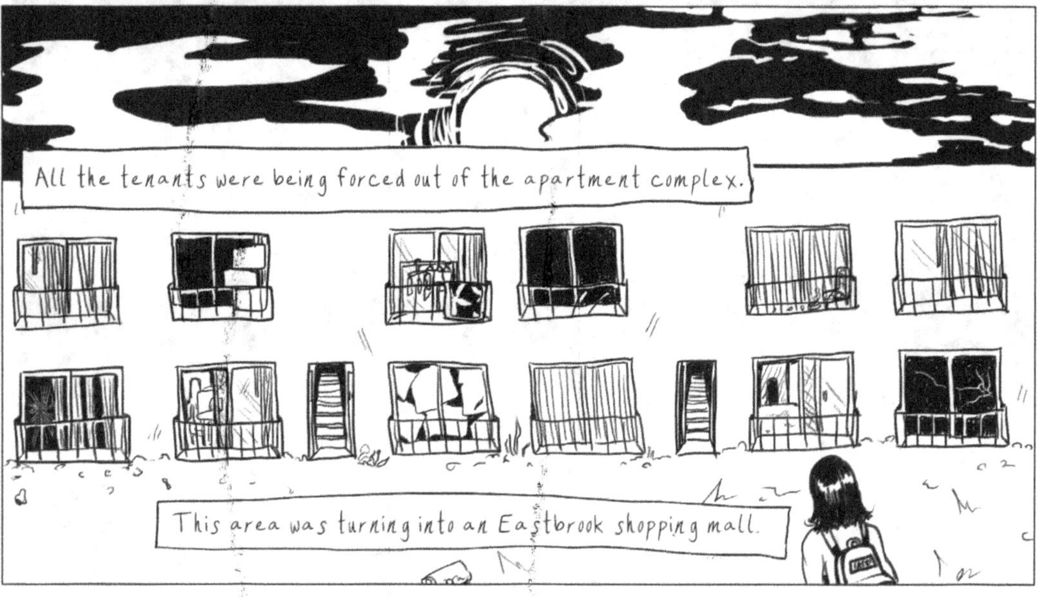
All the tenants were being forced out of the apartment complex.
This area was turning into an Eastbrook shopping mall.

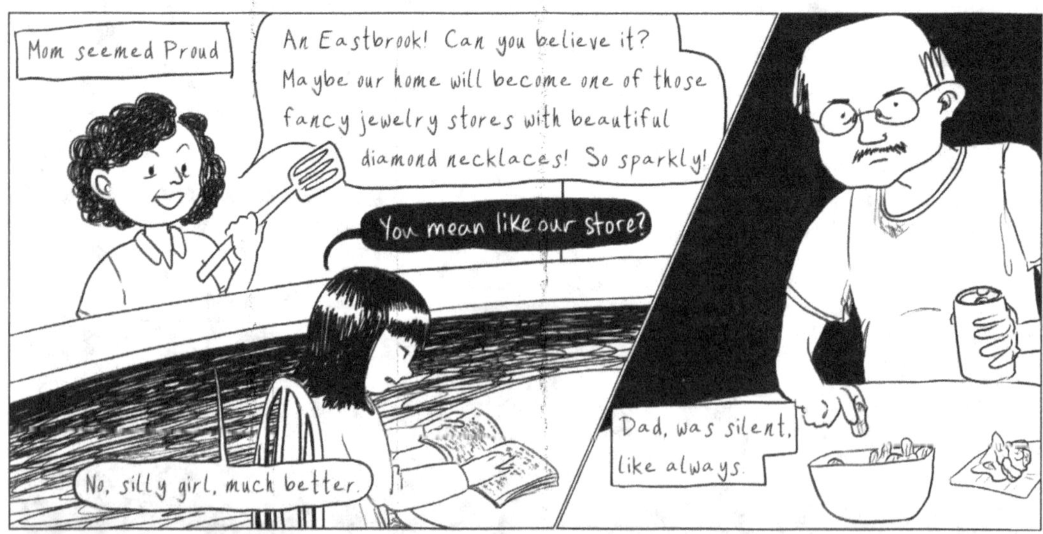
Mom seemed Proud
An Eastbrook! Can you believe it? Maybe our home will become one of those fancy jewelry stores with beautiful diamond necklaces! So sparkly!
You mean like our store?
No, silly girl, much better.
Dad, was silent, like always.

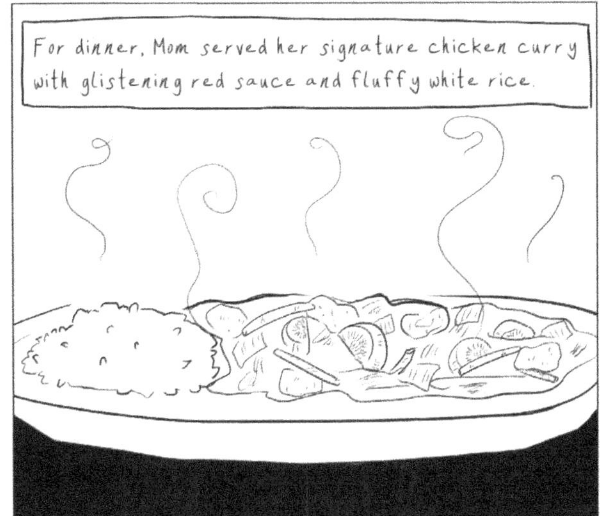
For dinner, Mom served her signature chicken curry with glistening red sauce and fluffy white rice.

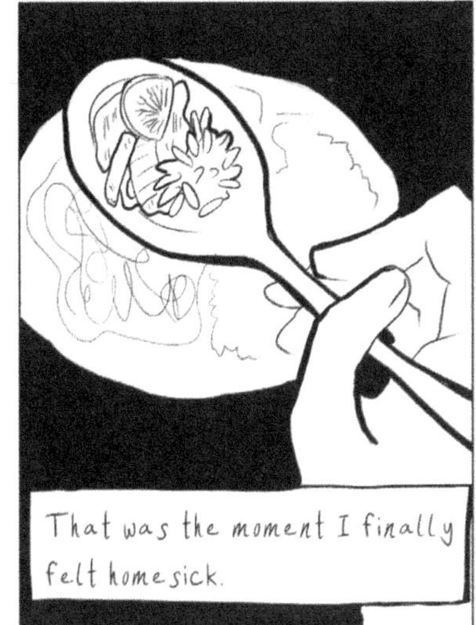
That was the moment I finally felt homesick.

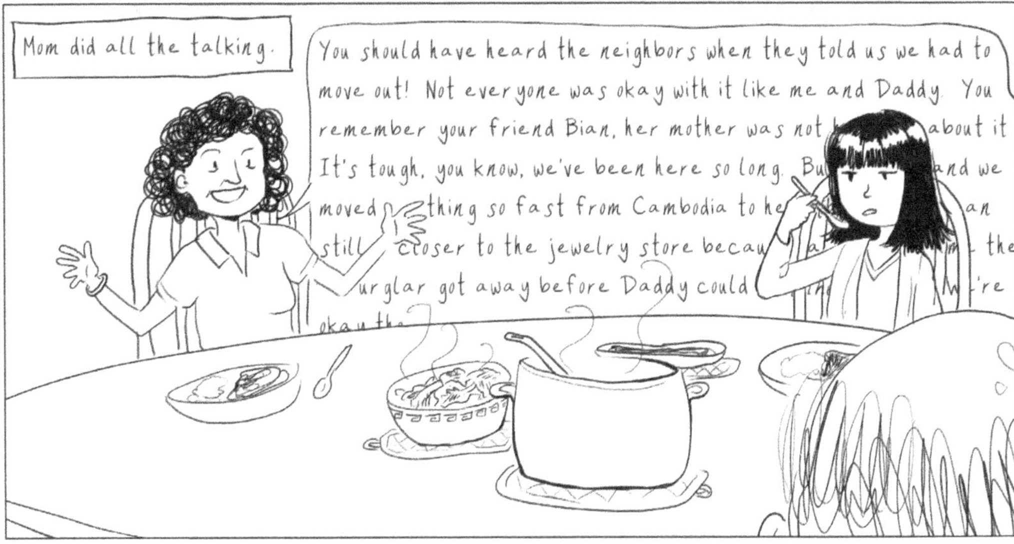
Mom did all the talking.
You should have heard the neighbors when they told us we had to move out! Not everyone was okay with it like me and Daddy. You remember your friend Bian, her mother was not about it It's tough, you know, we've been here so long. and we moved thing so fast from Cambodia to still closer to the jewelry store the got away before Daddy could

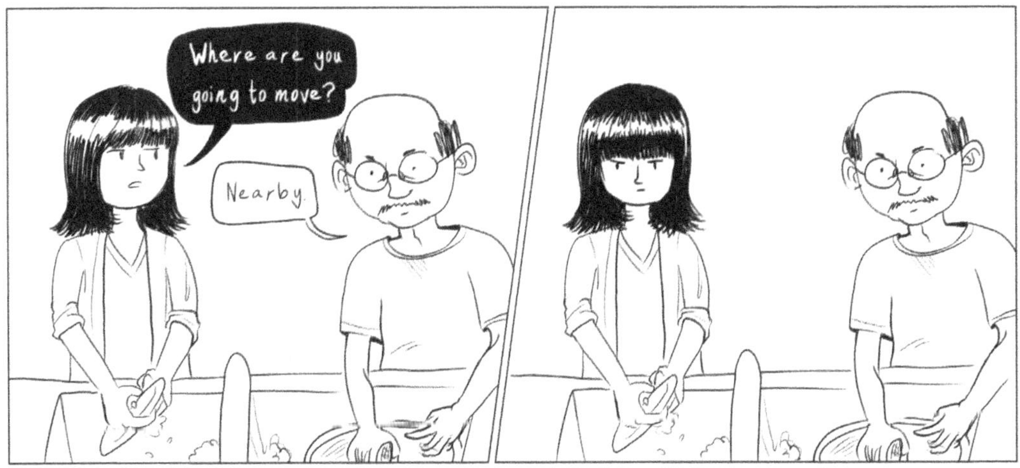
Where are you going to move?
Nearby.

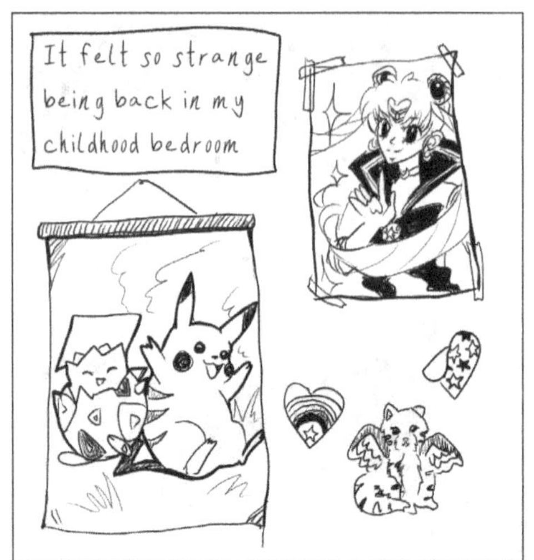
It felt so strange being back in my childhood bedroom

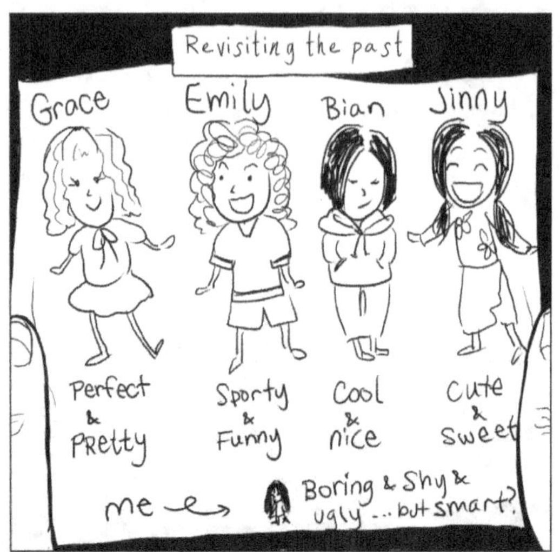
Revisiting the past
Grace
Emily
Bian
Jinny
Perfect & Pretty
Sporty & Funny
Cool & nice
Cute & sweet
me
Boring & Shy & ugly ... but smart?

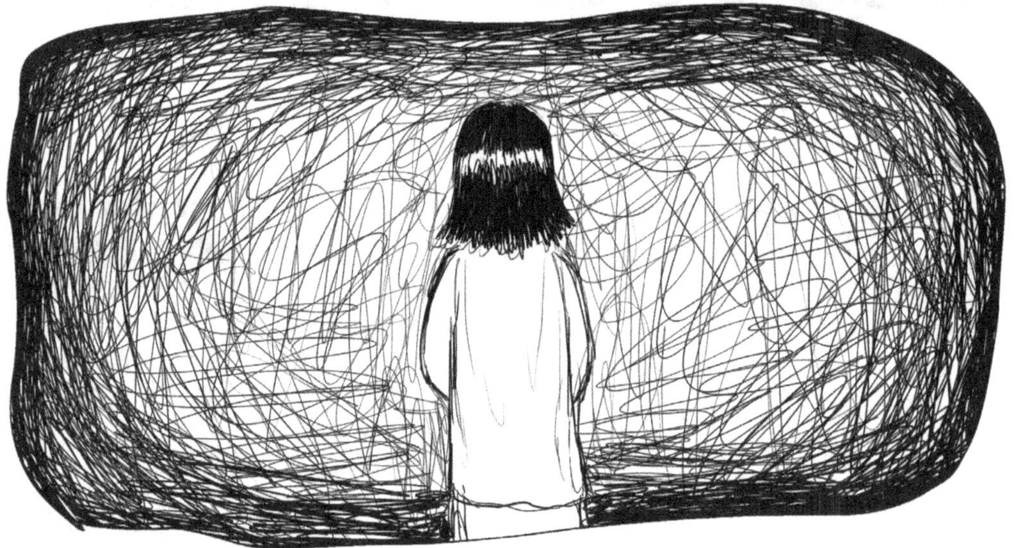

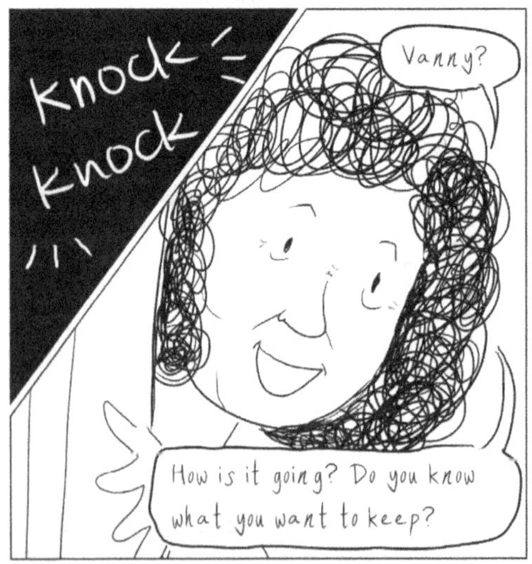
knock knock
Vanny?
How is it going? Do you know what you want to keep?

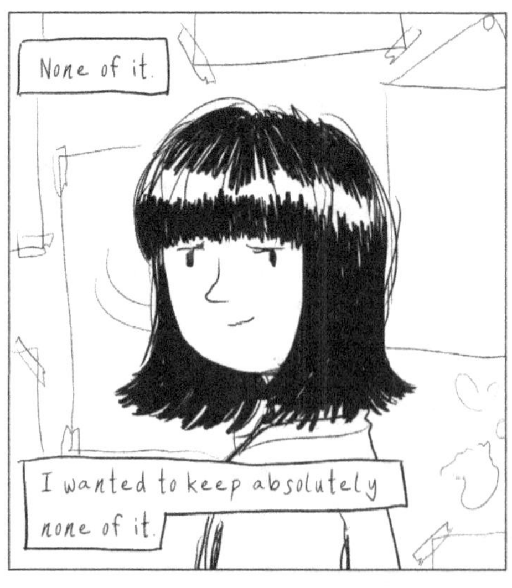
None of it.
I wanted to keep absolutely none of it.

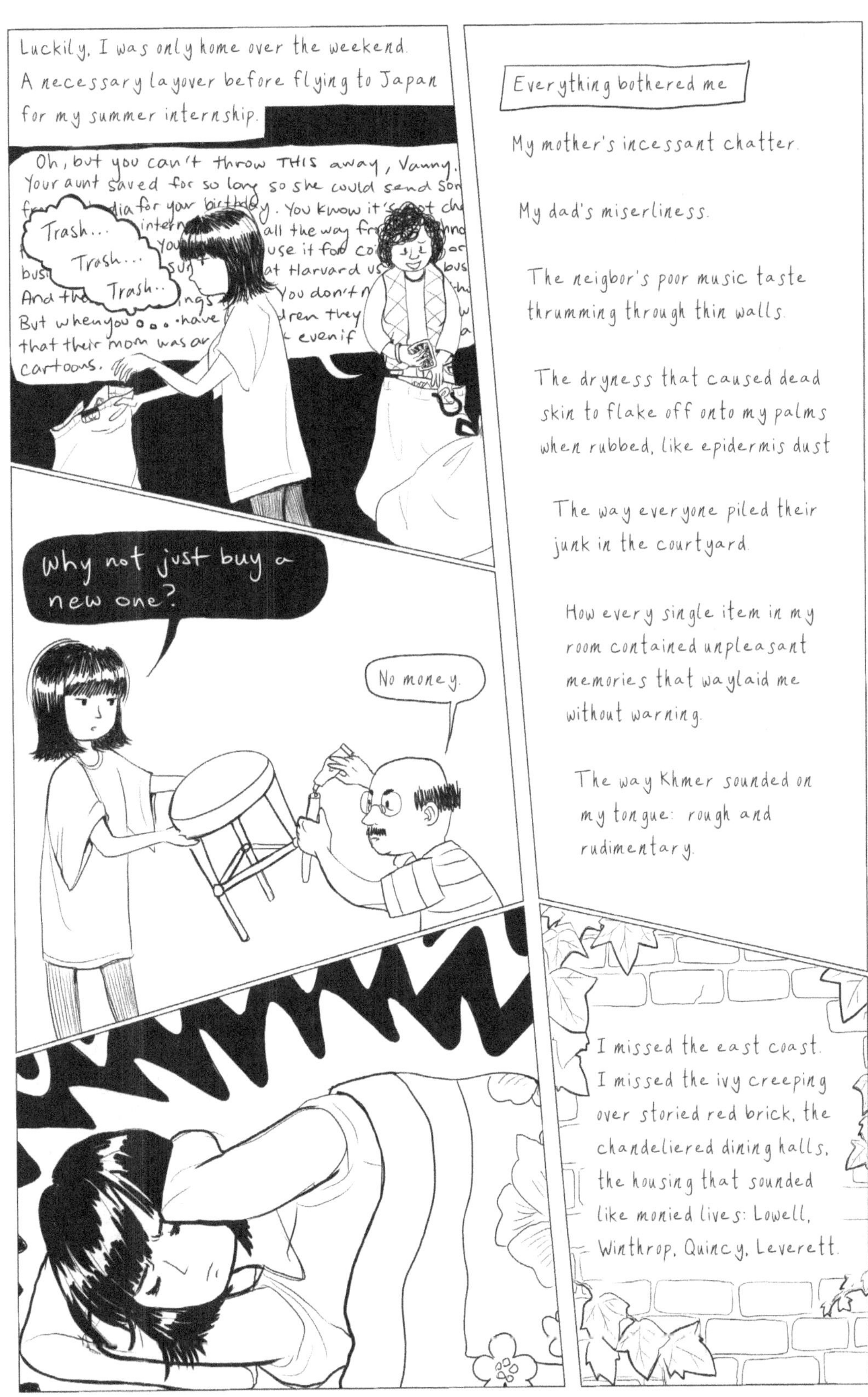

Luckily, I was only home over the weekend. A necessary layover before flying to Japan for my summer internship.
Oh, but you can't throw THIS away, Vanny.
Trash... Trash... Trash...
Why not just buy a new one?
No money.
Everything bothered me
My mother's incessant chatter.
My dad's miserliness.
The neigbor's poor music taste thrumming through thin walls.
The dryness that caused dead skin to flake off onto my palms when rubbed, like epidermis dust
The way everyone piled their junk in the courtyard.
How every single item in my room contained unpleasant memories that waylaid me without warning.
The way Khmer sounded on my tongue: rough and rudimentary.
I missed the east coast. I missed the ivy creeping over storied red brick, the chandeliered dining halls, the housing that sounded like monied lives: Lowell, Winthrop, Quincy, Leverett.

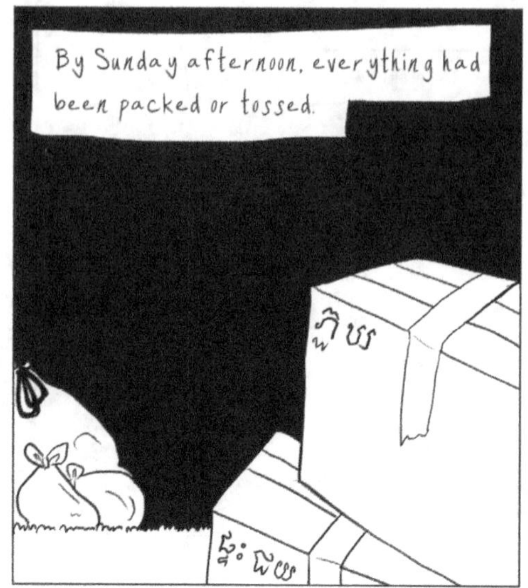

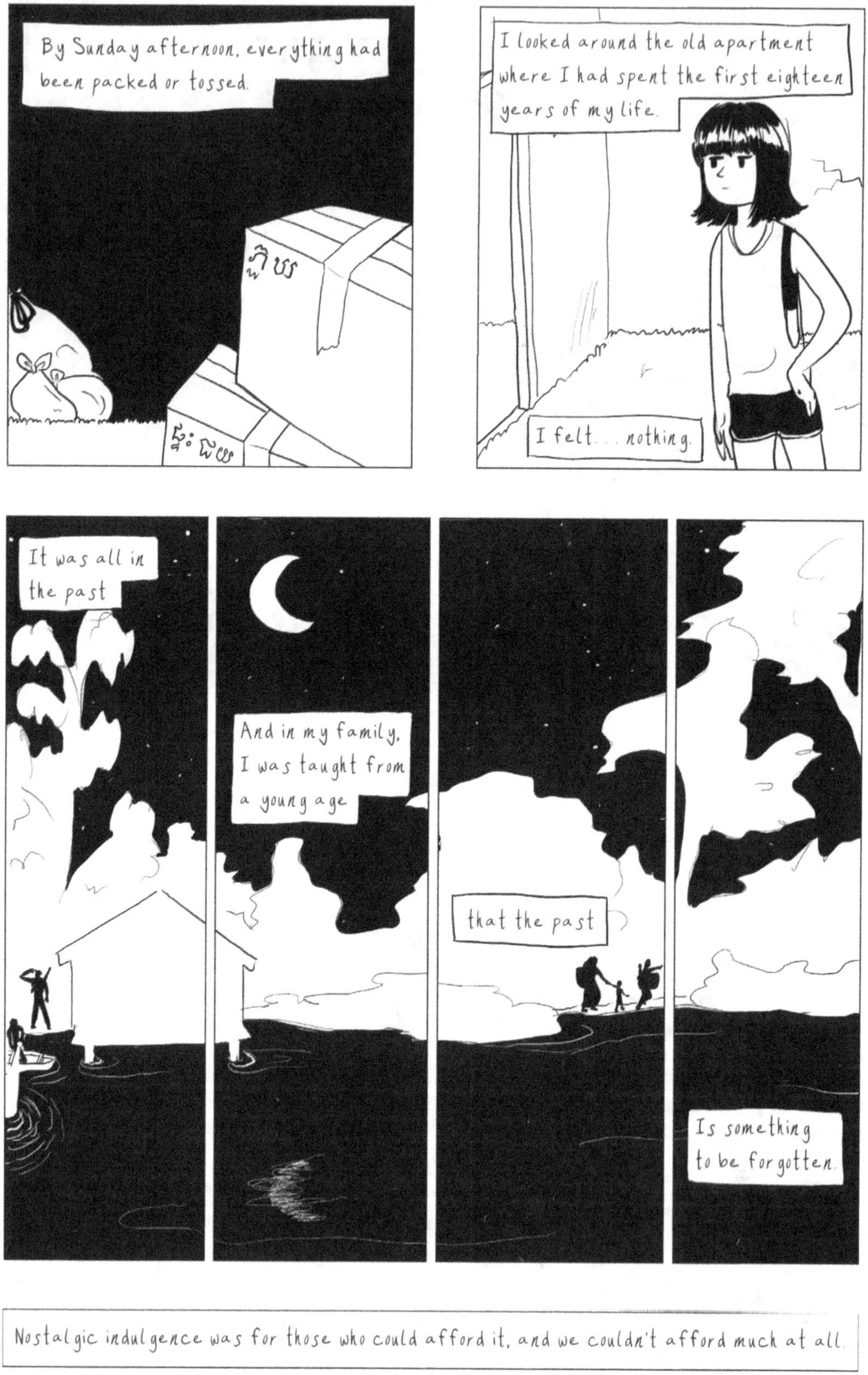

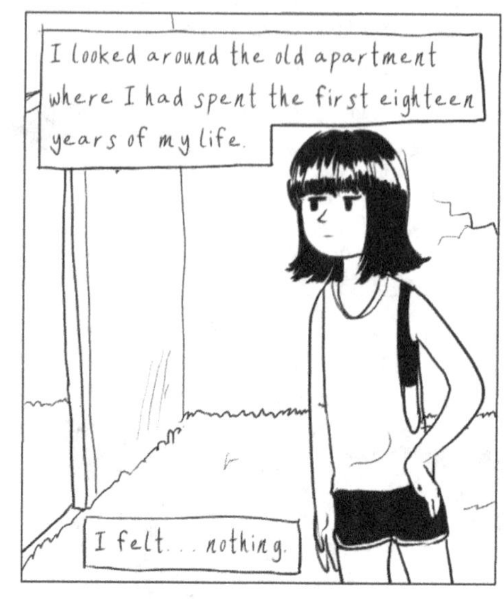

It was all in the past

And in my family, I was taught from a young age

that the past

Is something to be forgotten.

Nostalgic indulgence was for those who could afford it, and we couldn't afford much at all.

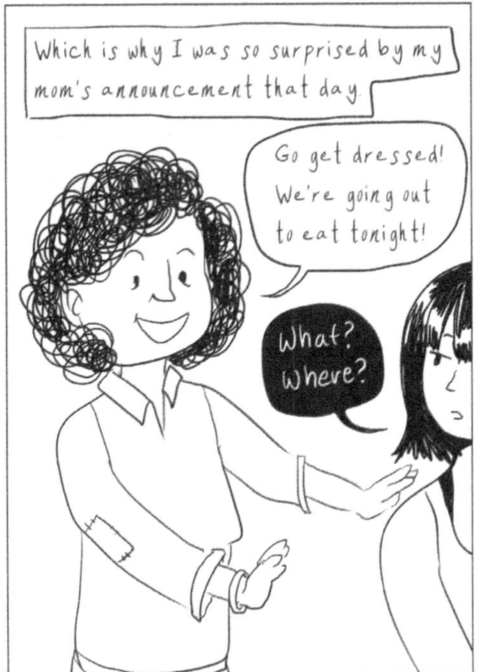

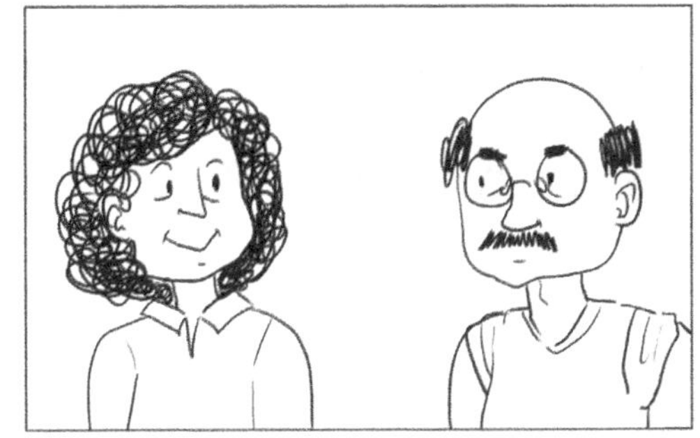

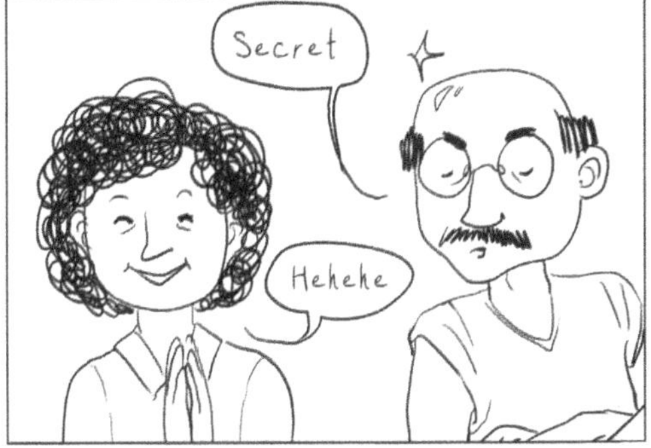

My parents put on their "best" clothes that had not changed for the last two decades.

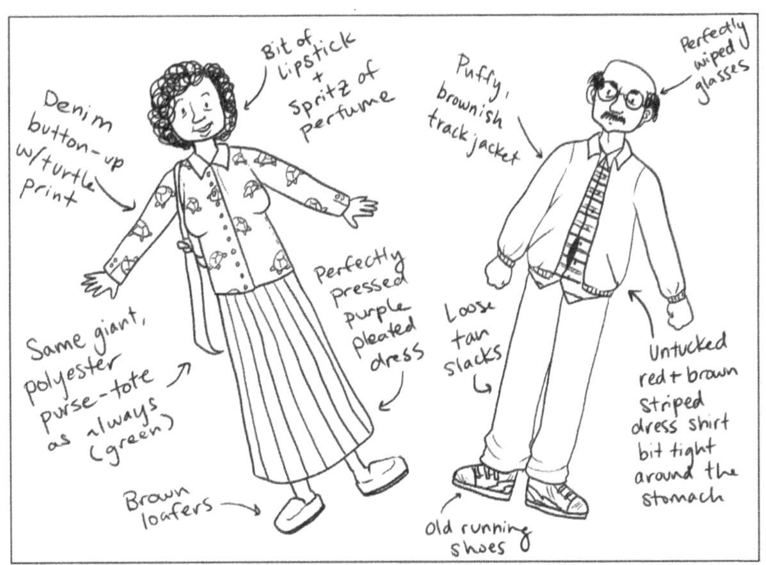

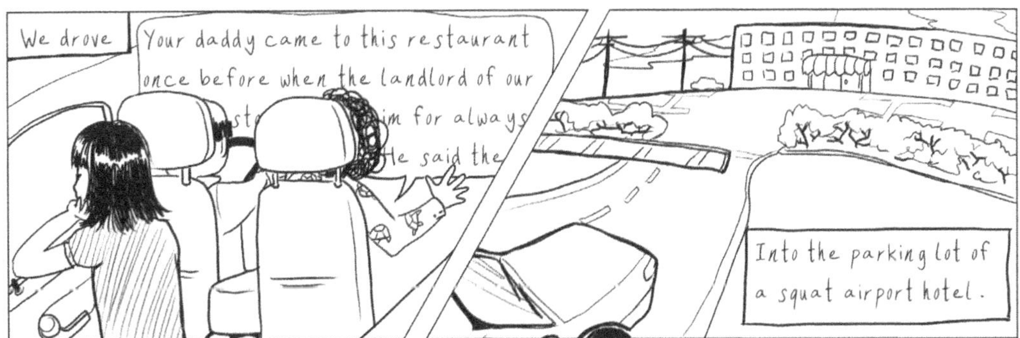

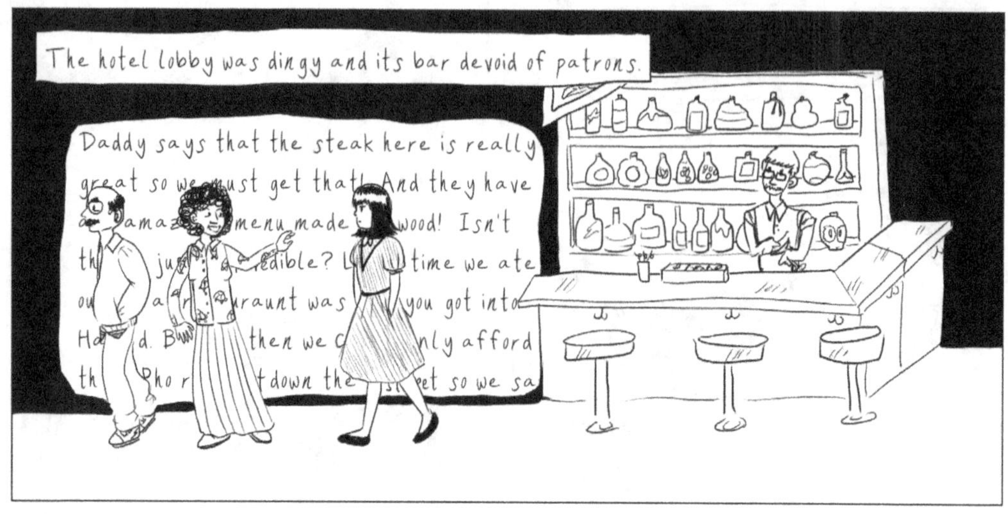
The hotel lobby was dingy and its bar devoid of patrons.
Daddy says that the steak here is really great so we must get that! And they have amaz menu made wood! Isn't th ju edible? L time we ate ou a r aurant was you got into Ha d. B then we c nly afford th Pho r t down the et so we sa

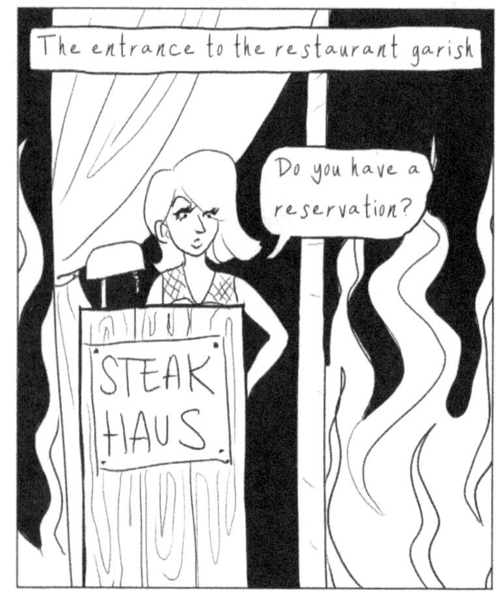
The entrance to the restaurant garish
Do you have a reservation?
STEAK HAUS

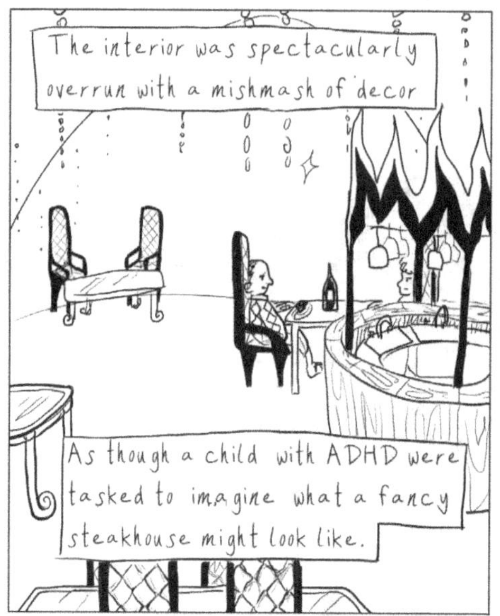
The interior was spectacularly overrun with a mishmash of decor
As though a child with ADHD were tasked to imagine what a fancy steakhouse might look like.

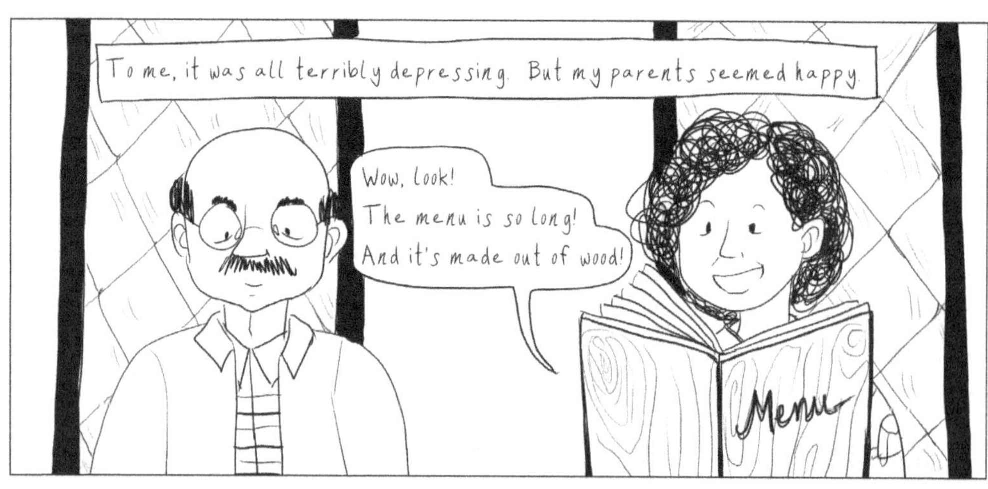
To me, it was all terribly depressing. But my parents seemed happy.
Wow, look! The menu is so long! And it's made out of wood!
Menu

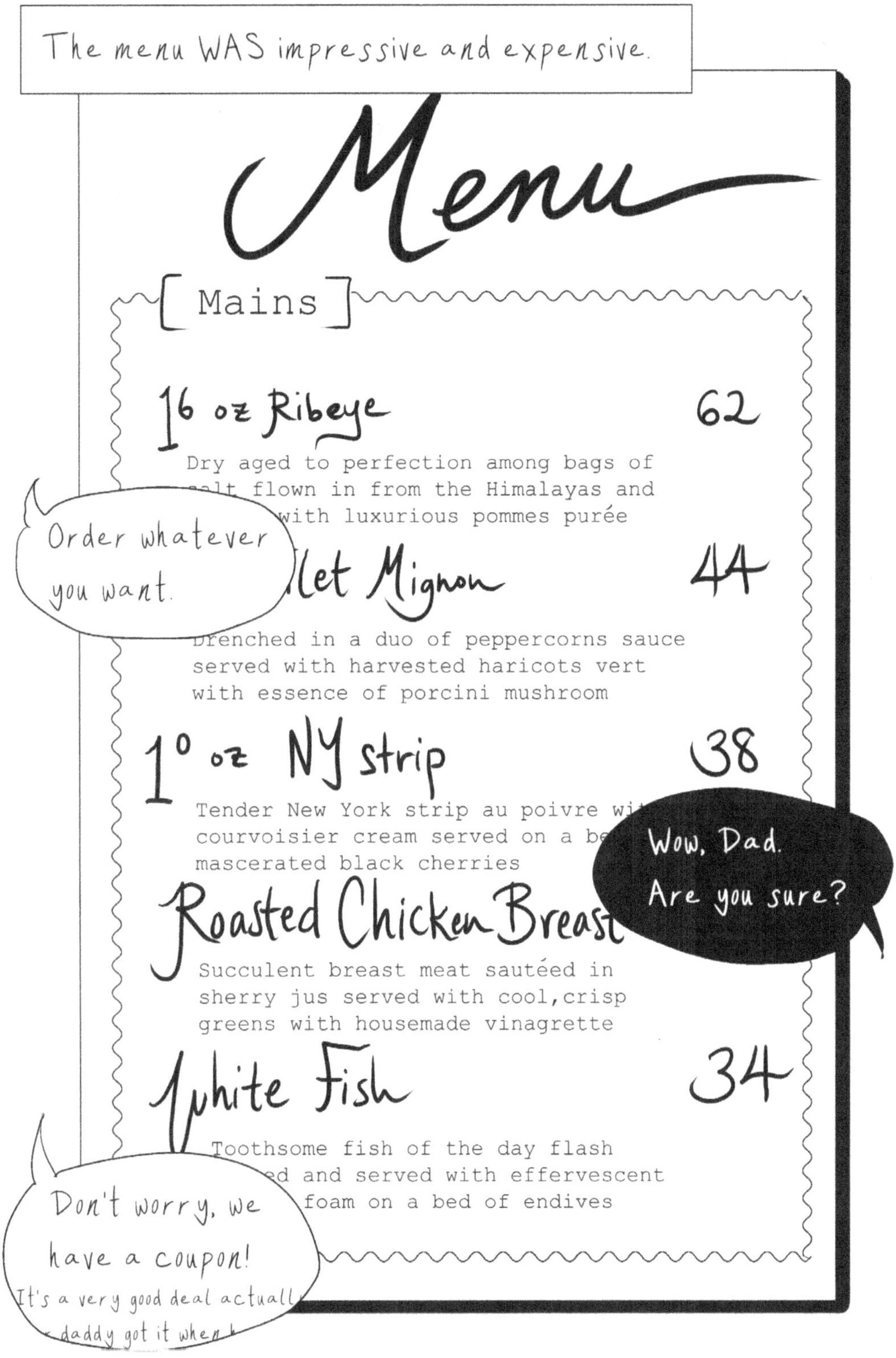

The menu WAS impressive and expensive.

Menu

[Mains]

16 oz Ribeye 62

Dry aged to perfection among bags of
alt flown in from the Himalayas and
with luxurious pommes purée

Order whatever
you want.

let Mignon 44

renched in a duo of peppercorns sauce
served with harvested haricots vert
with essence of porcini mushroom

10 oz NY strip 38

Tender New York strip au poivre wi
courvoisier cream served on a be
mascerated black cherries

Wow, Dad.
Are you sure?

Roasted Chicken Breast

Succulent breast meat sautéed in
sherry jus served with cool,crisp
greens with housemade vinagrette

White Fish 34

Toothsome fish of the day flash
ed and served with effervescent
foam on a bed of endives

Don't worry, we
have a coupon!
It's a very good deal actuall
daddy got it when

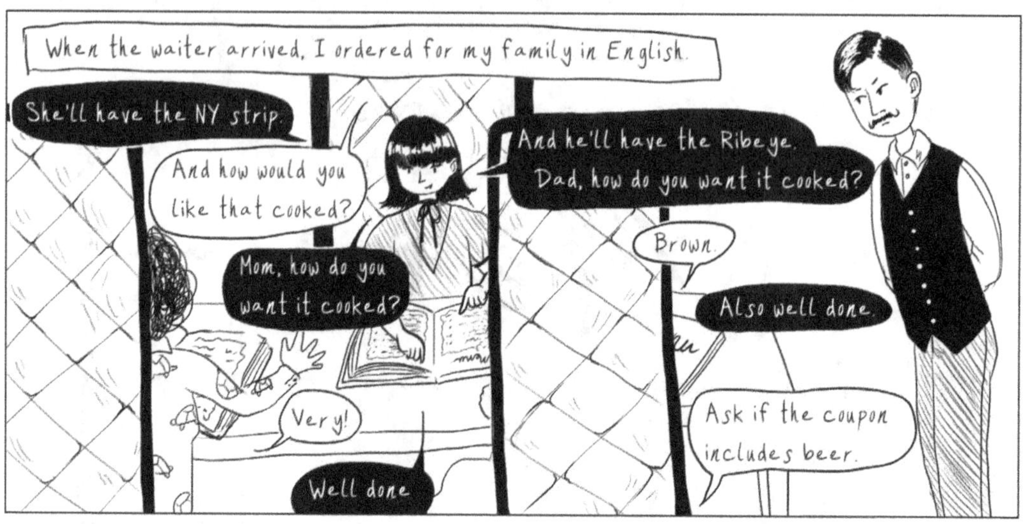
When the waiter arrived, I ordered for my family in English.
She'll have the NY strip.
And how would you like that cooked?
Mom, how do you want it cooked?
Very!
Well done
And he'll have the Ribeye. Dad, how do you want it cooked?
Brown.
Also well done.
Ask if the coupon includes beer.

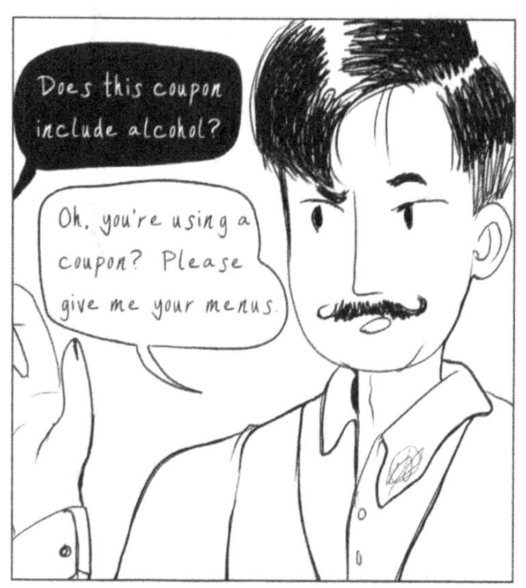
Does this coupon include alcohol?
Oh, you're using a coupon? Please give me your menus.

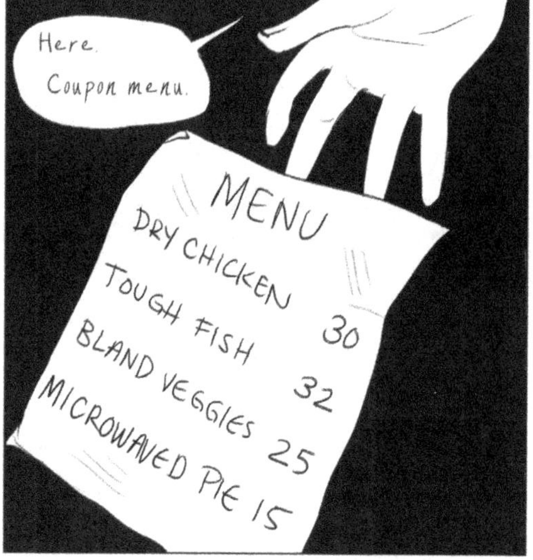
Here. Coupon menu.
MENU
DRY CHICKEN 30
TOUGH FISH 32
BLAND VEGGIES 25
MICROWAVED PIE 15

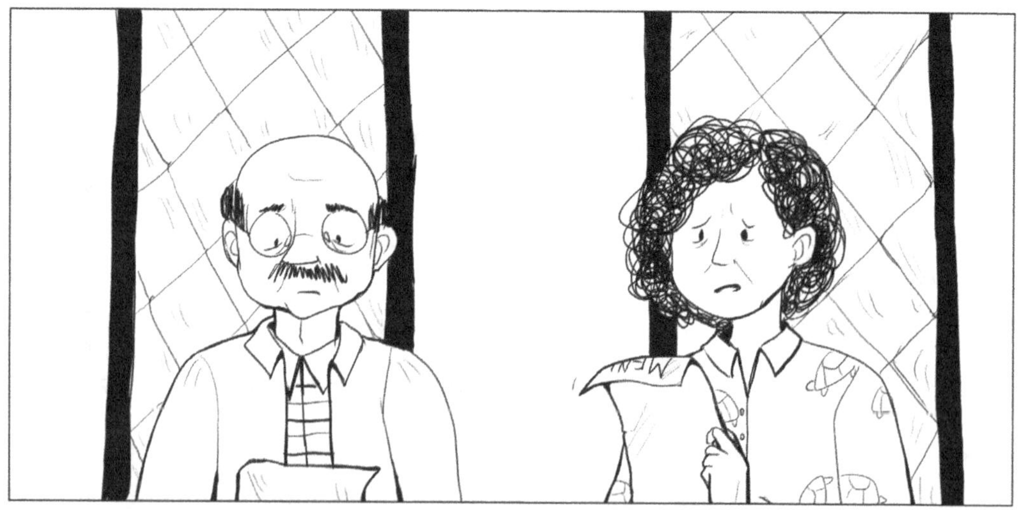

I don't remember what I ordered. All I remember is that it wasn't very good.

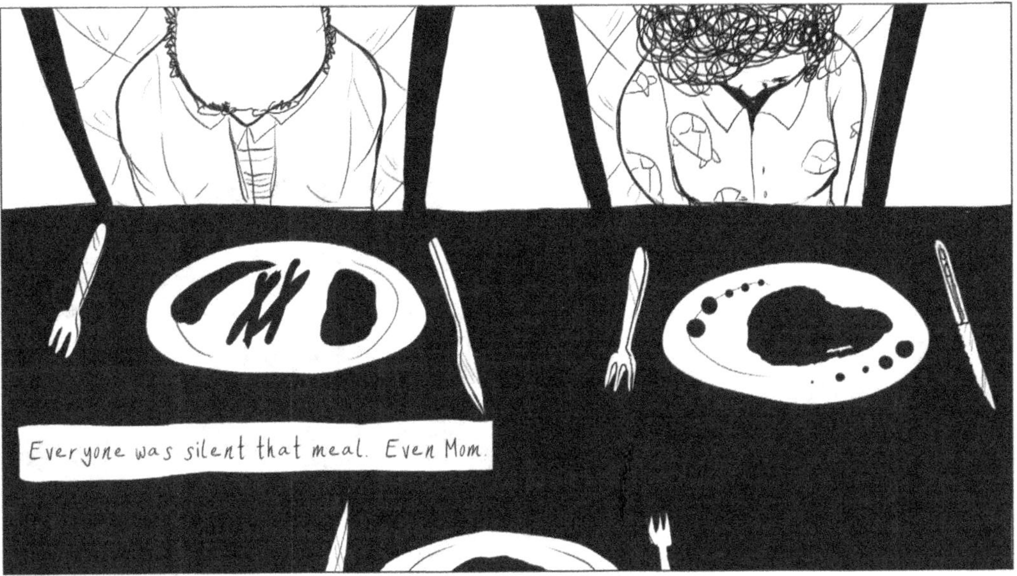

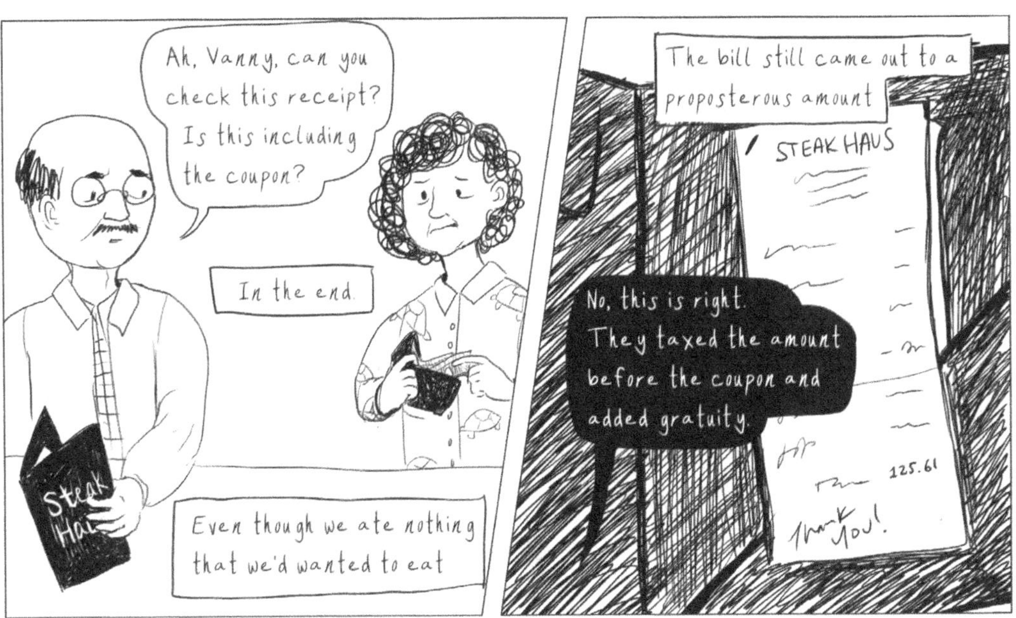

It was a tense ride home. All I could think about was leaving for Japan the next day.

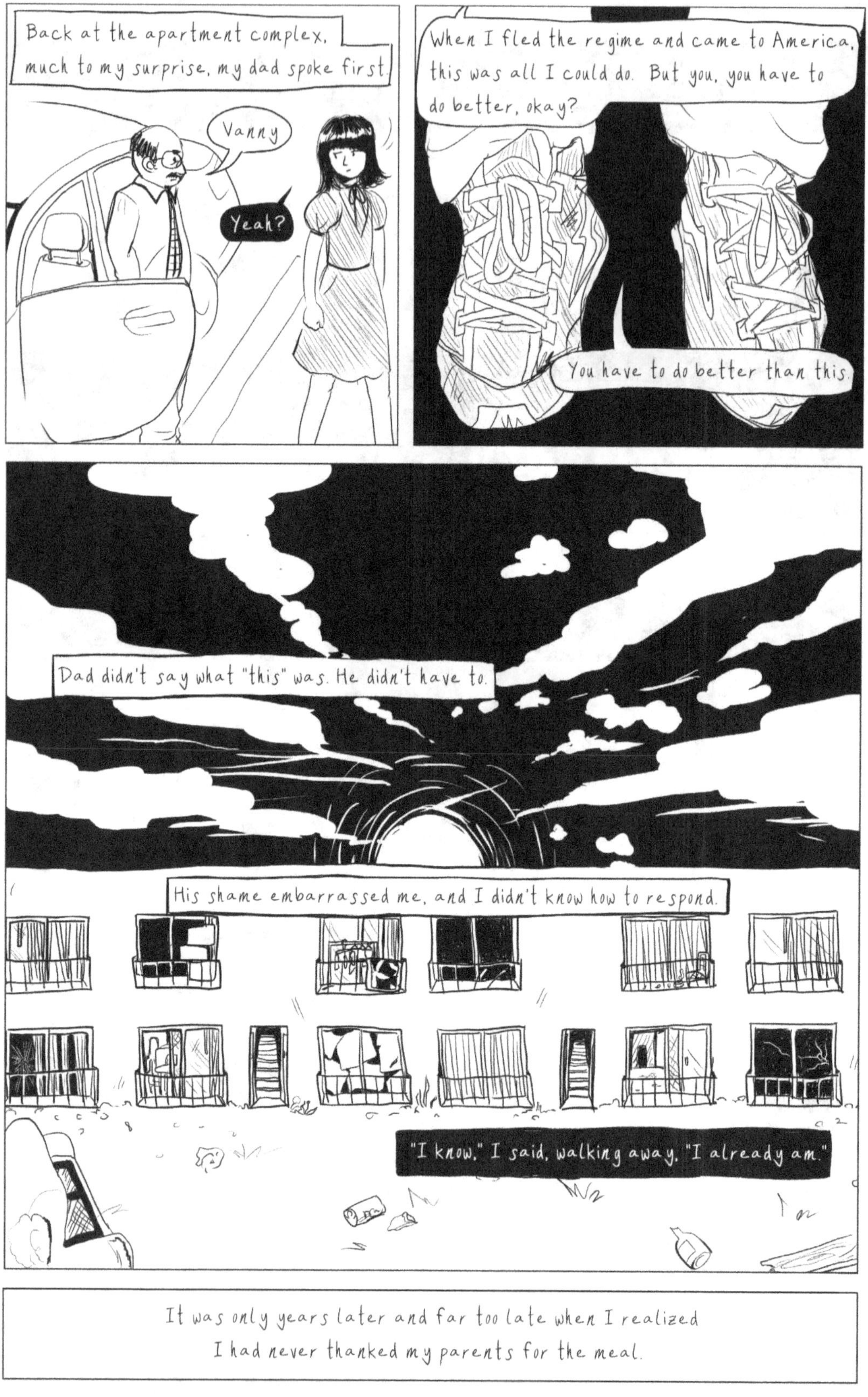

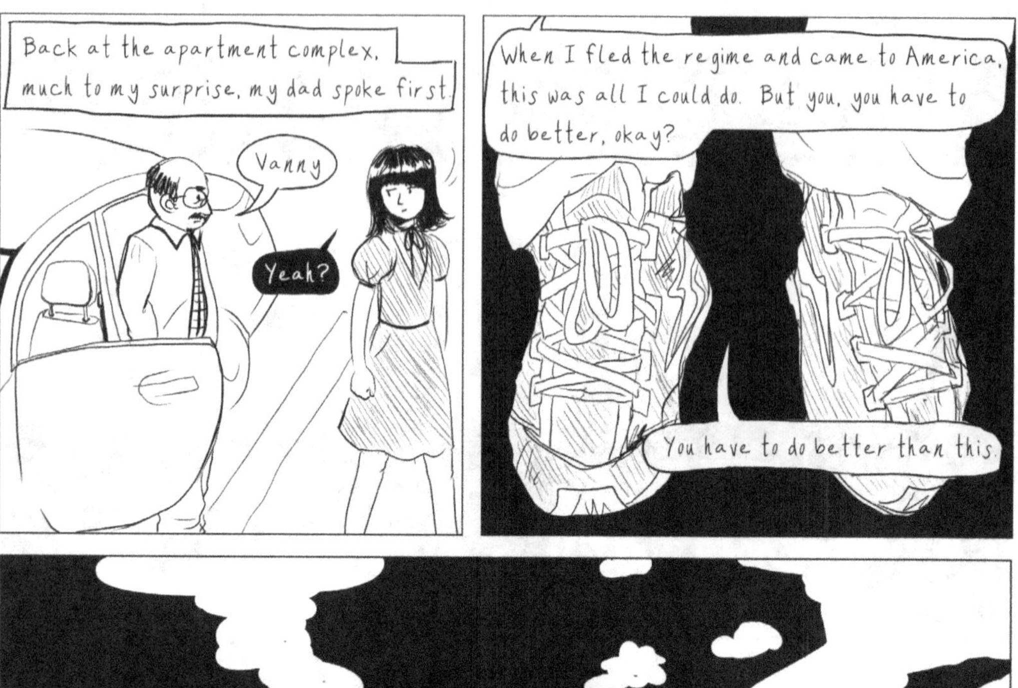

Dad didn't say what "this" was. He didn't have to.

His shame embarrassed me, and I didn't know how to respond.

"I know," I said, walking away. "I already am."

It was only years later and far too late when I realized
I had never thanked my parents for the meal.

INTERVIEW
WITH KAT Y. TANG

When did you create "Paper Menu"?

That's actually an interesting question because "Paper Menu" is a story I've come back to time and time again. I have a document that's titled "Paper Menu (rewrites)" with one version of the story written in 2018 and then a completely different version in 2019. This version, from 2020, is the first time I've told the story in comic form instead of as a short story and somehow that made all the difference!

Did you have a difficult time deciding on whether to add a title to your work?

I knew what the title of the work would be, but I didn't know whether or not to have a full title page. Ultimately, I was struck by the simple power of a white on black title page.

Perhaps the harder decision, though, was whether or not to have my name on the title page. While writing and drawing the comic (which is part of a larger novel), I envisioned that this was a comic created by Vanny a few years after the events of this story when she's had a bit of time to reflect. Therefore, I actually considered penning in Vanny as the author. But as a stand-alone piece, I think that would have been too confusing, so I used my name instead. But in the novel, I will probably put Vanny's name or leave the name off entirely so the reader can draw their own conclusions about the authorship of the comic.

"Paper Menu" is a powerful lens into family dynamics. Which parts of this story were the easiest to translate into a comic? Which were the hardest?

Since "Paper Menu" is part of a longer novel, I've had a lot of time thinking about things, like how the apartment complex looked and what sorts of interests Vanny would have had growing up. The other girls in the drawing Vanny picks up—Emily, Grace, Bian, and Jinny—are characters whose POVs you get in the rest of the novel. Actually, that panel was such a mindfuck (am I allowed to say fuck?) because it was me drawing Vanny drawing herself looking at a drawing that I drew of her drawing of her childhood drawing. Say that ten times fast.

The harder part to translate into comic form was the way characters related to each other. In prose, you can use lengthy narrative to tell the reader what the dynamic is between characters. But with a comic, where visuals and not words are prioritized, that has to be done through other means. I think character placement on the page helped (how far apart did they sit or stand from each other in the panel?) as well as establishing routine interactions in the earlier pages.

Artists and writers are always evolving and improving their craft. What are some choices you made in "Paper Menu" that differ from previous work?

This is actually the first full graphic narrative I've ever drawn, so it was really fun for me, as someone who's currently at an MFA program for more traditional prose writing, to play around with a different form.

Just like characters can be crafted in written language through a well-chosen word, comics are amazing because you can change a character with a single line. I found it so fun to play around with the nuances of expression and also the juxtaposition of words and drawings: are they telling the same story? Different stories? Is the character lying to herself, to the audience? Why? What does Vanny the "author" want and how is that conveyed through Vanny the "character"?

What do either of them get? As a professor of mine often said, "the difference between what the character wants and what the character gets is story."

There are several moments in the comic where speech bubbles are obscured by a character in the foreground, adding layers of complexity and character building to this intimate story. Is this a technique you have used before? What do you think can be gained in these moments where parts of the dialogue might be lost?

I think because drawing comics is new to me, it's easier to break with convention because I don't really know what convention is! Generally, I felt more free to do what fit the needs of the characters. That's why Vanny's dialogue bubbles are in black and Vanny's mother's dialogue runs on and on and is often obscured by other characters (often Vanny herself). Kids often tune out what their parents say, and since the story is told from Vanny's perspective, we get what she hears and not the whole story, even if we as readers might want to know the full extent of what her mother is saying! I tried to leave enough in so that an interested reader might be able to piece it together if they wanted to.

What font do you use for the dialogue? Outside of the consistency, it almost appears handwritten. What do handwritten fonts add to a text—especially one narrated as yours is?

My handwriting is exceptionally awful, so I had to create a font based off of my handwriting so that it would be consistent and legible enough to read!

I also wanted the whole comic to have an intimate feel to it, almost claustrophobically so, hence why I chose not to use standard fonts. The only place where you see a standard font is with the "fancy" menu and I think it adds to the feeling of this meal being something beyond their means.

What was the hardest part of crafting the piece?

My back! Hunching over a Cintiq (drawing tablet) for hours every day takes its toll on you physically. But in all seriousness, I think it was evoking emotions through characters that felt human, which is really what I endeavor for in all my work.

Planning out the frames ahead of time and pacing the story was definitely the hardest part for me because I'm used to doing that with words and not with frames and images. It's also much more time consuming to redraw frames than to rewrite prose!

Transitioning from creating artwork to fully-fledged comics can often feel daunting for artists. Do you have any tips for aspiring comic writers? What were things you wish you would have known when you were starting out?

I'm not sure I'm the most qualified to be giving tips, but, this is my first full-fledged comic and it's now published with *Driftwood Press*! So I guess my tip would just be to go for it! You never know what's been brewing for years that's just waiting to turn itself into a comic or short story or interpretive dance or whatever amazing form. Just be open to the possibilities.

Also, remember that completing a project is an achievement worth celebrating. That's something I tell myself so that I actually complete any one of the ten projects I'm always starting at the same time.

What other mediums have influenced your work? How?

I'm a staunch believer that everything in life, especially if it's creative, can fuel your work. I've dabbled in a myriad of creative outlets: break dancing, pottery, graphic design, piano, graffiti stenciling, DND, painting, weaving, and so on. There are certainly principles that apply across artistic pursuits, and especially ideas around space, contrast, and surprise are ones that I got from other artistic fields that I thought about a lot as I was working on this comic.

What are your own artistic goals for the future? Simply, what do you want to do next?

Now that I've written one comic, I'm excited to try out more (maybe with color next time?). I'm also, as I mentioned above, working on a novel that's mostly traditional prose, with the exception of "Paper Menu." Hoping to get a first draft of that done some time this year and then publish my first book!

Contributors

Mason Boyles is a first-year PhD student in FSU's creative writing program. He holds his MFA from UC Irvine, where he received the Weinberg and Schaeffer Fellowships. His fiction has appeared in publications such as *The Wisconsin Review, The Baltimore Review, The New Guard,* and *Black Dandy*, among others. He is currently revising a novel about a set of un-conjoined twins who inherit a system of folk magic and a collapsing Appalachian strip mine.

Lynda Montgomery's fiction has appeared in *december magazine* and *Another Chicago Magazine.* She's attended residencies for fiction at the Vermont Studio Center, Ragdale Artist Community, and the Virginia Center for the Creative Arts. The Ohio Arts Council awarded her an Individual Excellence Award in 2020 for fiction.

Robin Gow (they/them or ze/hir) is a trans and queer poet and young adult author. They are the author of *Our Lady of Perpetual Degeneracy* (*Tolsun Books,* 2020) and the chapbook *Honeysuckle* (*Finishing Line Press,* 2019). Gow's first Young Adult book is forthcoming Winter 2022 with *FSG Books for Young Readers.* Their poetry has recently been published in *POETRY, New Delta Review,* and *Washington Square Review.*

Lora Kinkade is a queer, rural poet residing in Mendocino, California. She received her B.A. in Creative Writing from the University of California, Santa Cruz. She was a founding member of the *Omni Writing Collective.* Her most recent publications include *Ursus Americanus Press, The Bombay Gin,* & *Matchbox Magazine.* She was a runner-up in *Omnidawn*'s 2018 Single Poem Broadside Contest.

Lina Patton is a graduate of George Mason's MFA program, where she was awarded the Thesis Fellowship in Fiction and served as fiction editor of the literary journal, *Phoebe.* Her novel excerpt was published in *Narrative Magazine* after placing as a finalist in its 2017 30 Below Contest and her work received an honorable mention from *Glimmer Train.* She also has work published in *Sweet* and *The Rupture.* She is working on a novel.

R.C. Davis is a high school junior from Oak Park, Illinois. He is a 2019 winner of the Gwendolyn Brooks Youth Poetry Awards, and his poems have been published in *3Elements Review* and *Blue Marble Review.*

Summer J. Hart is an interdisciplinary artist from Maine, living in the Hudson Valley, New York. Her written and visual artworks are influenced by folklore, superstition, divination, and forgotten territories reclaimed by nature. She is the author of the micro-chapbook, *Augury of Ash* (*Post Ghost Press,* 2020). Her poetry can be found in *Waxwing, The Massachusetts Review, Denver Quarterly, Northern New England Review,* and elsewhere. Her mixed-media installations have been featured in galleries including Pen + Brush, NYC; Gitana Rosa Gallery at Paterson Art Factory, Paterson, NJ; and LeMieux Galleries, New Orleans, LA. She is a member of the Listuguj Mi'gmaq First Nation. You can find out more about Summer on her website (summerjhart.com).

Ben Kline lives in Cincinnati, Ohio. His chapbook *SAGITTARIUS A** landed in October 2020 from *Sibling Rivalry Press.* A poetry reader for *The Adroit Journal* and *Flypaper Lit*, he is the 2020 recipient of the Christopher Hewitt Award for poetry, as well as a finalist for both the 2020 Donald Hall Prize for Poetry and the 2020 National Poetry Series. His work can be found in *The Cortland Review, Lunch Ticket, No Contact, DIAGRAM, Hobart, Juked, A&U Magazine,* and many other publications. You can read more on his website (benklineonline.wordpress.com).

BRENNAN MCMULLEN is a recent graduate of Boston University, where they polished their predilection of poetry with the school's highly inclusive spoken word club. Their writing often addresses mental health and oppressive systems. They enjoy protests and computer programming. More of their work can be read on their website (mothwash.github.io).

WREN HANKS is the author of *The Rise of Genderqueer,* a 2018 selection for *Brain Mill Press*' Mineral Point Poetry Series. A 2016 Lambda Literary Emerging Writers Fellow, his poetry has been a finalist for *Indiana Review*'s 1/2 K Prize and anthologized in *Best New Poets.* His recent work appears or is forthcoming in *Indiana Review, Waxwing, Third Coast,* and elsewhere. His new manuscript, *Lily-livered,* was a finalist for *DIAGRAM*'s 2020 chapbook contest. He is also the author of *Prophet Fever* (*Hyacinth Girl Press*), an Elgin Award finalist. He lives in Brooklyn, where he is a supervisor for ACC's New Hope program, a proactive community initiative that finds homes for vulnerable dogs, cats, and wildlife.

KELSEY M. EVANS is a young artist and designer from Salt Lake City. She is inspired by the natural world and surrounds herself with plants, music, and animals. Kelsey likes to combine color and create texture in her work as a way to express emotion, movement, and spirit. In the past, Kelsey has illustrated multiple books including a series used to teach women's health with the non-profit group Healthy Am I. She is drawn to projects that focus on making the world better and hopes to continue creating designs and illustrations for meaningful causes. Find her on Instagram (@kelseymariestudio) or at a local artisan market around Austin, TX.

SAM HEYDT works across different media, including film, video, installation, photography, sculpture, sound, and text. Heydt presents an abstract proposition for a world on the periphery of history, one that not only appears haunted by the ghosts of the past, but built on it. Conflating time and place, her layered imagery collides, merges and disrupts logical relationships between occurrences. Through adding and subtracting meaning by combining images of destruction with portrayals of the virtues born from the American Dream, Heydt confronts the disillusionment of our time with the ecological and existential nightmare it is responsible for.

JAKE GOLDWASSER is a linguist, cartoonist, and poet based in Brooklyn. You can find his work in *The New Yorker, Weekly Humorist, The Spectacle, The Meadow,* and elsewhere. Jake's artwork and writing explore humans' changing relationship with language, the environment, and the future. He is a New Jewish Culture Fellow for the 2020-2021 cycle, for which he is teaching a graphic novels workshop. You can find more about him on his website (jacobgoldwasser.com).

KAT Y. TANG is a life-long doodler who has arrived at fiction by way of law. She is currently a Fiction MFA student at Columbia University. Born in Hangzhou, China, Kat has relocated across several continents and now lives in Manhattan, NYC. Her work explores themes of belonging and family and what we do when we think no one is watching. Her short stories have received honorable mentions in *Pigeon Pages* and *Momaya Press.* She is working on a mixed prose-comic novel.

www.ingramcontent.com/pod-product-compliance
Lightning Source LLC
Chambersburg PA
CBHW080520030726
47592CB00012B/3418
* 9 7 8 1 9 4 9 0 6 5 0 9 1 *